Walther Ziegler

Wittgenstein
in 60 Minutes

Translated by
Alexander Reynolds

My thanks go to Rudolf Aichner for his tireless critical editing; Silke Ruthenberg for the fine graphics; Lydia Pointvogl, Eva Amberger, Christiane Hüttner, and Dr. Martin Engler for their excellent work as manuscript readers and sub-editors; Prof. Guntram Knapp, who first inspired me with enthusiasm for philosophy; and Angela Schumitz, who handled in the most professional manner, as chief editorial reader, the production of both the German and the English editions of this series of books.

My special thanks go to my translator

Dr Alexander Reynolds.

Himself a philosopher, he not only translated the original German text into English with great care and precision but also, in passages where this was required in order to ensure clear understanding, supplemented this text with certain formulations adapted specifically to the needs of English-language readers.

What can be said at all can be said clearly and what we cannot talk about we must pass over in silence. [1]

Bibliographic Information held by the German National Library: The details of the original German edition of this publication are held by the German National Library as part of the German National Bibliography; detailed bibliographical data can be found online at www.dnb.de.

© 2019 Dr Walther Ziegler
1st Edition December 2019
Jacket design and graphic design for the whole book: Silke Ruthenberg, making use of illustrations by:
Raphael Bräsecke, Creactive – Studio for Advertising, Comics & Illustrations
© JackF - Fotolia.com (image-frames)
© Valerie Potapova - Fotolia.com (image-frames)
© Svetlana Gryankina - Fotolia.com (speech-balloons)

Publisher and Printing:
BoD – Books on Demand, Norderstedt
ISBN 978 3750426955

Contents

Wittgenstein's Great Discovery

Ludwig Wittgenstein (1889-1951) is known as the great pioneer of what is called "linguistic philosophy" and counts, for this reason, among the most powerfully influential thinkers of the 20th century. The "linguistic turn" that he initiated was an epoch-making turning point in human culture: the turn, specifically, of philosophy away from its traditional focus on such topics as "being" and "consciousness" toward a concern above all with language.

Whereas, before Wittgenstein, the answer given to the question as to "the meaning of life" had tended to be a speculative or a materialistic one – one couched in terms of the "self-unfolding of the World-Spirit", the "development of human history through class struggle", or "the will to power" – Wittgenstein turned, for the first time, to consider language as the most important phenomenon shaping and forming human life. Language – so ran Wittgenstein's core insight – is absolutely decisive for our understanding of the world.

This, Wittgenstein's discovery of language as that through which all knowledge of the world is focussed put into question all philosophy prior to his day. Because, as Wittgenstein now argued, quite regardless of what it was that each individual philosopher, from antiquity up to Wittgenstein's own day, may have recognized to be "essential reality", it is and remains a fact that these philosophers could acquire their respective insights into this "essential reality" always only within the limits set by language. Except by means of words and verbal propositions, he pointed out, no philosopher, nor indeed any human being, is able to form any meaningful thought at all:

The limits of my language mean the limits of my world. [2]

There is in the end no escape from the "cage of language", no matter how hard one might try to conceive, even once, of a thought without recourse to words or sentences:

> This running against the walls of our cage is perfectly, absolutely hopeless.[3]

Even the common saying "one's thoughts are one's own" expresses only a subjective illusion because thoughts can only ever be expressed through language. Beyond language there is nothing:

> When I think in language, there aren't 'meanings' going through my mind in addition to the verbal expressions: the language is itself the vehicle of thought.[4]

For language to be the "vehicle" of our thought means that everything, absolutely everything that goes on in our head – every notion, every insight and every idea – comes to pass only in and through words and sentences. We begin to learn language already in our earliest childhood and from this point on language determines our whole perception of the world and everything that we know about it. This is why, so argues Wittgenstein, the first and most important task of philosophy consists in finally setting about analysing and understanding language as the most basic tool of all its knowledge. We need to find out what mankind can logically grasp by means of language and what it cannot. Because it is only in this way that it is possible to distinguish false and meaningless statements about the world from meaningful ones:

All philosophy is a 'critique of language'. [5]

For thousands of years, Wittgenstein contended, philosophers had done nothing but build mental constructions that were open to misunderstanding or even self-contradictory without first having clarified the logical preconditions of what they were doing:

> Most of the propositions and questions of philosophers arise from our failure to understand the logic of our language. [6]

By finally setting about analysing this "logic of language", he went on, and achieving understanding of what can meaningfully be said and what cannot, the multitude of philosophical problems are either demoted to the modest rank they deserve or even dissolved altogether:

> A whole cloud of philosophy condensed into a drop of grammar. [7]

And indeed with this demand that philosophers finally set about examining language itself Wittgenstein inspired new philosophical currents all over the world: "ordinary language philosophy" in England; "speech act theory" and the "theory of communicative action" in Germany; structuralist "semiotics" in

France; the Neo-Positivist philosophy of the Vienna Circle in Austria; and the "theory of linguistic relativity" in America.

But Wittgenstein's discovery of the great significance of language has not been without consequence even for our daily lives. Whereas for centuries language had been looked upon merely as a direct means for human beings to make themselves understood, today it is deployed in a targeted manner to influence private and public discourses and to manipulate entire forms of life. An army of communication coaches, marketing strategists and political consultants tries, day by day, to influence our reality by the targeted use of words and phrases. Be it in the form of advertising or propaganda campaigns, speech therapies, self-motivation courses or prayer meetings – it is only since Wittgenstein that language has been recognized for what it really is, namely a force field which reflects, but also influences, our lived reality in its entirety:

The speaking of language is part of an activity, or of a life-form. [8]

Wittgenstein himself wanted only to analyze language, never to instrumentalize it. He even warned against its instrumentalization. Nonetheless, with his discovery of the connection between language and life-form he opened, one might say, Pandora's Box. Once the profound significance of language for our daily life was recognized, efforts were made to a greater degree than ever before to manipulate human beings by targeted use of language.

Today, Wittgenstein's name is normally mentioned beside those of Kant, Heidegger or Sartre, even though he was, initially, sharply critical of philosophy and had planned originally to become an engineer. One might even say that he became a philosopher "despite himself". The eighth child of the leading Austrian steel magnate Karl Wittgenstein, his interests lay initially in the direction of technology and mathematics. Like his father before him, he did his university studies in the field of engineering.

But in the midst of making the calculations needed for a new aeroplane motor he was suddenly, against all his plans, seized with such a passion for philosophical questions that his sister became worried for his health. "At this time," she later wrote, "Ludwig was suddenly consumed, powerfully and against his own will, by meditations on philosophical problems so that he began to suffer severely from the inner conflict between this vocation and the vocation he had already resolved upon [...] All through this period he was constantly in an indescribable, almost pathological state of excitement." [9]

The young Wittgenstein simply had no choice, then, but to pose to himself the great philosophical questions: What is the world? How can I know it and make true statements about it? From this point on he devoted himself entirely to the study of the logicians Frege, Russell and Moore. And already before he had completed this second self-formation in philosophy he was able to propose to the world, in his *Tractatus Logico-Philosophicus*, an answer. This small treatise comprised barely eighty pages, something more than unusual for a work of philosophy. But it made Wittgenstein famous already in his own lifetime.

The secret of the *Tractatus*'s success, which it would doubtless have enjoyed at any point in philosophical history, lies in its razor-sharp structure. Like a surgeon with a scalpel Wittgenstein answers the question "what is the world?" in seven theses that follow logically on from one another. He numbered these like Bible verses, expanding each of them with equally rigorously sequentially numbered sub-theses, so that the general impression made by the book's seven strictly scientific theses was that of a dogmatic or even messianic proclamation. Starting from his core idea that all our knowledge of the world must necessarily be formulated in words and sentences, Wittgenstein goes on to explain, point by point, how human beings can produce absolutely correct and indubitable propositions about this world. Henceforth, he concluded, the scientist may formulate only propositions which make logical sense and can be checked against and confirmed by reality. All other propositions he must recognize to be literal "nonsense" and refrain from enunciating. This is the gist of the final often-cited seventh thesis of the *Tractatus*:

> What we cannot speak about we must pass over in silence. [10]

This final thesis was so provocative because it permitted, basically, the enunciation of no propositions at all about the world except the propositions of the natural sciences and thus invalidated philosophy entirely:

> The correct method in philosophy would really be the following: to say nothing except what can be said, i.e. propositions of natural science [...] [11]

For Wittgenstein, then, philosophy was bound to "pass over in silence" even such matters as had always traditionally belonged to its domain as questions of justice and of ethics. Because one can never check and confirm, experimentally, against reality such moral propositions as "You must not steal" or "You should act always only in such a way that the maxim of your action might be expanded to become a law that is valid for all", since such propositions refer to the future and are thus by their very nature insusceptible of such checking and confirming:

> So too it is impossible for there to be propositions of ethics. [12]

By declaring in this way, in his *Tractatus*, all those questions and theories that could not be answered and demonstrated in natural-scientific terms to be literal "nonsense" the young Wittgenstain believed that he had rid both the world and himself, once and for all, of the tormenting problems of philosophy:

I [...] believe myself to have found, on all essential points, the final solution of the problems.[13]

But this was not the end of the story. Wittgenstein was later himself to call into question the rigorous position that he had taken up in his first book. After five years working as a schoolteacher in rural Austria he made a second discovery about language, this one of even broader ramifications. Language, as he came to observe among his pupils, certainly does not, in its daily use, serve the one narrow purpose of describing what he had called in the *Tractatus* "states of affairs", let alone the even narrower one of distinguishing scientifically between correct and incorrect propositions. In its everyday use language is utilized in a much more various and extensive way. For example to announce one's intentions, or to wish, to promise, to command, to threaten, to curse, to praise, to exhort, or to demand – in short, as a way of bringing about actions to be performed by oneself or by others. These observations led Wittgenstein to his famous theory of "language-games" which was expounded in a larger book published only after his death under the title *Philosophical Investigations*:

Look on the language-game as the *primary* thing. [14]

In the *Philosophical Investigations* Wittgenstein describes, for example, dissimulation, lying, mimicry, sign-language, emotional outbursts and numerous other phenomena of linguistic expression. The theory of "language-games" that emerges from these descriptions opens up entirely new dimensions as compared to the theory developed in the *Tractatus*. For this reason, a distinction is generally made between "the early" and "the late" Wittgenstein. In his late work Wittgenstein recognizes that it is always only the concrete "language-games" in which they occur – i.e. the innumerable everyday conversations that go on between children, workmen, theologians, scientists or football players – that give words their meaning. The "games" in question, he emphasizes, follow their own rules and conventions. Philosophical analyses of these "language-games" are so important because they serve to throw light on the atmosphere of these latter, that is to say, on the underlying "forms of life" of language's various speakers. This atmosphere, these "forms of life" Wittgenstein argues, often determine our sense of what it is we are living – that is to say, what counts as "reality" for us – far more than does any scientifically correct description of the world:

Put a man in the wrong atmosphere and nothing will function as it should [...] Put him back into his proper element and everything will blossom and look healthy. [15]

"Words can work miracles", it is commonly said. The opposite is also true: an apparently open conversation can be "poisoned" from the start by the language in which it is conducted. Wittgenstein's primary concern, indeed, was to analyse, describe and understand language-games, not to alter them or actively intervene in them. Just by discovering the connection, however, between language-game and lived reality he had pushed open, in fact, the door to an entirely new understanding of this reality.

Even in the great work of his "late period", the *Philosophical Investigations*, Wittgenstein holds true to the thesis he had advanced in the *Tractatus* whereby we know the world only within the limits of our language. In the later work, however, what concerns him is no longer the logically correct formulation of scientific propositions but rather the meaning of language as it is used in our daily lives. Because words and propositions are far more than just a means of describing things or coming to a practical understanding with others. These words and propositions, through their use, also give rise to entirely new meanings and these meanings both mould and are moulded by our respective "forms of life". Every human being, whether he or she be a scientist, a priest or an athlete, is constantly involved in a great multiplicity of language-games, all of which profoundly mark his or her thinking, perception of the world and form of life.

But if language marks and moulds our lives to this degree, if it really is a "cage" for all our thoughts and thinking, what becomes of human freedom? Do language-games really determine every aspect of our daily lives and the whole of our lived reality? And if so, of what use is Wittgenstein's discovery to us? Is it possible perhaps to change this lived reality by adopting a more careful use of language? Is language also used in order to manipulate?

Wittgenstein's view of the world was a view of such passionate clarity and rigour that it has still today lost none of its fascination.

Wittgenstein's Central Idea

What is the World? The World Consists Only of Facts Which We Picture to Ourselves in Propositions

Already the very first proposition of the *Tractatus*, that numbered with the single numeral "1", is of a spellbinding simplicity:

The world is all that is the case. [16]

One can hardly imagine a simpler statement. The world is, in the first instance, simply everything of which it can be said: "yes, such is indeed the case". It is, for example, "the case" that the earth is round, that it turns on its own axis, and that it exerts upon us its gravitational force. It is furthermore "the case" that it is surrounded by an atmosphere which enables us to breathe. Were these things not "the case", then we would asphyxiate, indeed, would fly off into outer space.

Thus far Wittgenstein's answer to the classical philosophical question "what is the world?" may seem banal, or just the repetition of something that goes without saying. So the world is simply "all that is the case"; the proposition appears true but trivial. But already in the first sub-thesis that he adds to this first main thesis – the proposition numbered "1.1" – he takes a step which carries his argument in a far from trivial direction:

The world is the totality of facts, not of things. [17]

In other words, from the point of view of the rigorous theory of knowledge that Wittgenstein is attempting to develop here, the world does not consist of the totality of all the "things" which might generally be believed to be "the case" but only of the totality of facts. That is to say, the world does not consist of the whole mass of ideas which have accumulated in our minds since our childhood and which we have subjectively held, at one time or another, to be "the case" – not, in other words, indiscriminately of all the traffic lights, automobiles, streets, guardian angels, mountains, forests, oceans and mermaids which we may, at one time or another, have held to be "things" – but rather only of the totality of the true "facts" that we know about the world and are capable of enunciating through language. This once specified, however, "guardian angels" and "mermaids" must be struck from the list we have just given. But how do we arrive at these "true facts"? How do they come to arise in our minds? Wittgenstein's answer is, once again, initially a very simple one:

We picture facts to ourselves. [18]

Biographers have often referred, in this context, to Wittgenstein's having followed with great interest a court case in which the judge had ordered the incident in legal dispute – a car accident – to be recon-structed in the court using small-scale models of the vehicles involved and dolls to represent their drivers. In this way the judge was able to clear away the contradictory accounts of events given by the parties to the case and form for himself a precise picture of what had really happened. Wittgenstein, it appears, was deeply impressed by this and it might even have been this that first inspired in him the "picture theory" that he later presented in the *Tractatus*. Because just like this judge – so argues Wittgenstein in his first philosophical work – human beings constantly, throughout their everyday lives, form pictures for themselves of reality so as to master the complexities and ambiguities of this latter and understand it better:

A picture is a model of reality. [19]

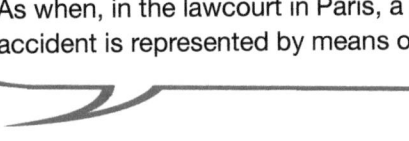

As when, in the lawcourt in Paris, a motor-car accident is represented by means of dolls etc. [20]

When I, for example, on seeing that the traffic-light is green, confidently walk across the road I have already formed for myself a picture or a model of the traffic-light's complex mode of functioning and of the entire traffic system associated with it. I have a model in my head that tells me that, as I walk, the same set of traffic lights will be sending a signal to the motorists involved in this situation to wait and not to advance, in such a way as to allow both pedestrian and vehicular traffic to proceed without problems. Of course, Wittgenstein adds, it is also possible for mistakes to be made here: i.e. for the picture or model of reality that one forms for oneself to not, in fact, match reality at all:

A picture agrees with reality or fails to agree. It is correct or incorrect, true or false […] There are no pictures that are true a priori. [21]

It is solely and exclusively the "correct" and "true" pictures of reality that can count as facts. But what is it, then, that distinguishes "facts" in this sense from illusions? Is, for example, the "guardian angel" not also a picture that we form for ourselves in our head? At this point Wittgenstein gives an answer of enormous consequence:

In order to tell whether a picture is true or false we must compare it with reality. [22]

This thesis is basically a reiteration of the principle that had set in motion the whole career of modern empirical natural science: namely, the principle whereby every picture, every model of reality and every hypothesis must necessarily be compared to this reality itself and be proven to concord with this latter by repeated experiments. This checking and comparing against reality is important. Without it, we might spend our whole lives forming pictures of the world that were mostly incorrect ones. In the next step of his argument Wittgenstein says that words and the propositions made from them are also, in the last analysis, pictures of the world that we experiment at putting together:

In the proposition a world is, as it were, put together experimentally. [23]

He also refers at this point to the hieroglyphic writing of the Egyptians:

In order to understand the essential nature of a proposition we should consider hieroglyphic script which depicts the facts that it describes. [24]

Chinese characters too, still today, are in many cases direct depictions of the facts that they represent. In Chinese script a drawing of a roof with the stylized image of a woman drawn underneath it still has the significance "peace". The same image of a woman drawn twice, but without a roof, means "pretty", while this image drawn three times, still roofless, signifies "conflict and strife". Since the very earliest times, then, human beings have been forming pictures of reality by means of words and propositions:

A proposition is a picture of reality. A proposition is a model of reality as we imagine it. [25]

But a proposition is only a proposition about real facts in the case where the picture formulated in and through the proposition in question is a picture which actually concords with reality. The proposition: "there are guardian angels and mermaids" would, for example, not be a picture of facts because, when compared and checked against reality, it would prove to be false.

Furthermore, statements about reality need not only to be checkable against this reality but also of such a form that they make logical sense. For example, if I say: "either it is raining outside just now or it isn't raining outside" this does, indeed, meet the condition just stated of being an empirically testable proposition, since I can simply stick my hand out the window to test whether it is in fact raining or not. But it remains nonetheless a proposition which contributes nothing to knowledge since it will be true in every possible state of affairs and is, consequently, arbitrary and void of any actual significance.

On this basis the Wittgenstein of the *Tractatus* advances his second great requirement for any viable theory of knowledge. All propositions which convey actual knowledge about the world – which concern, that is to say, actual "facts" – must display a logical structure and must not, on analysis, prove to be literal "non-sense".

Propositions About Facts Must Make Sense!

Wittgenstein now does something fascinating. In the further course of the argument developed in the *Tractatus* he sketches out scenarios in which all logically possible and conceivable propositions are examined with a view to their scientific usability. There are, he argues, in the whole world only sixteen so-called "truth-operations" – that is to say, only a very limited number of possible propositions through which facts can be expressed. These are "and" propositions, "if-then" propositions, "or" propositions, "not" propositions, "neither-nor" propositions and so on. One can, for example, say: "a tree is not made of metal" or "if an object is made of nothing but metal, then it is not a tree". Wittgenstein now sets about examining the claims to validity implicitly raised by such propositions with a view specifically to finding out the "general logical form of the truth-function" to which all these propositions can be analytically boiled down. The result he arrives at is the following:

The general form of a proposition is: this is how things stand. [26]

By saying this Wittgenstein is saying that every proposition – regardless of which of the sixteen possible propositional constructions or "truth-functions" we happen to be using in any particular case – serves, in the last analysis, always one and the same end: the description of an object or an event. But not every proposition in which one describes "how things stand" is necessarily scientifically usable:

A proposition states something only in so far as it is a picture. [27]

Wittgenstein now sets about analysing which types of propositions are such that they can describe real facts and which are not. Here, he arrives at the conclusion that there are, essentially, three different types of proposition: *meaningful, meaningless* and *nonsensical.* The only one of these three proposition-types that is useful for science is, of course, the meaningful proposition, because it is only this latter that pictures a fact in such a way that the reality of the fact can be checked and confirmed:

[...] We can simply say: 'This proposition represents such and such a situation'. [28]

As *meaningless*, by contrast, Wittgenstein classifies all propositions that are either *tautological* or *contradictory*. The term tautological comes from a composite construction in Ancient Greek: *tauto logia*, "the logic of the same thing" or, more loosely translated, "the repetition of what one has said already". Examples of tautological propositions would be: "the grey horse is grey" or "In wet weather conditions the weather conditions are wet".

Likewise scientifically *meaningless*, Wittgenstein goes on, are *contradictory* propositions. These propositions are useless as valid knowledge-claims because they involve, within a single proposition, two claims which are in fact not logically reconcilable with one another. Examples would be: "The teacher draws a square triangle", "the winner of the race came in second" or "I see a green dot that is red":

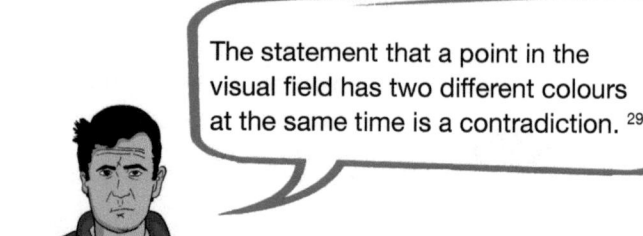

The statement that a point in the visual field has two different colours at the same time is a contradiction. [29]

To sum up, then: to form a tautological proposition is to describe something which will always necessarily be identical with the thing to be described and will thus in all circumstances be true; to form a contradictory proposition is to describe something which cannot possibly exist and will thus in all circumstances be false:

Thus, neither [the tautology nor the contradiction] can determine reality in any way. [30]

Tautological and contradictory propositions are thereby *meaningless*. Interestingly, however, Wittgenstein also points up a third type of proposition which is also, like the tautological and the contradictory, unfit to be used in the project of acquiring scientific knowledge. These are the propositions that he calls *nonsensical*. Wittgenstein designates as "nonsensical" the type of proposition which, without being either tautological or contradictory, is nonetheless unable to give to its propositional content any concretely graspable sense nor, consequently, any real "meaning":

> [...] If [a proposition] has no sense, this can only be because we have failed to give a *meaning* to some of its constituents. [31]

A statement which is, in the terminology developed by Wittgenstein in the *Tractatus*, not *meaningless* but rather *nonsensical* would be, for example, the statement "the cause of all life on earth is God", since this statement does not in fact ascribe to "life on earth" any truly concrete cause or meaning. The meaning which, in this statement, is assigned to all living beings – namely, "God" – is in fact no meaning at all. This is because it is uncheckable against reality, since God, according to Wittgenstein, necessarily "lies outside of the world". Science, however, is justified in ascribing to whatever it refers to *only* those meanings which lie "inside the world", that is, which can be clearly articulated and checked against reality:

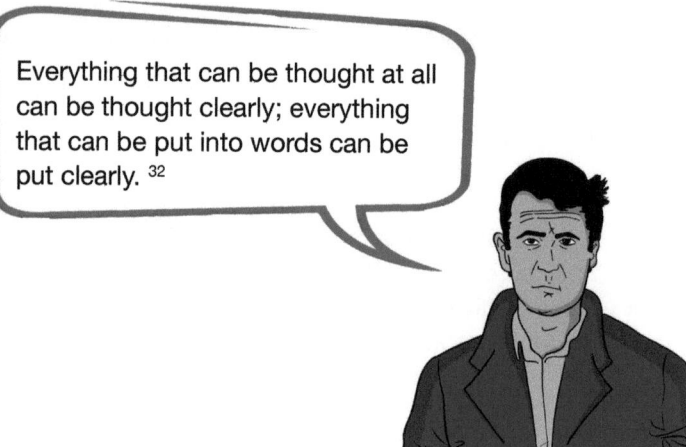

Everything that can be thought at all can be thought clearly; everything that can be put into words can be put clearly. [32]

To sum up, then: The world is all that is the case. What "is the case", however, is not all those pictures that we happen to make for ourselves of the world but only the facts. These "facts which are the case" can only be expressed by the scientist in the form of propositions. But the scientist can make use, in doing so, only of propositions which, firstly, make logical sense and, secondly, are such as to be able to be checked against reality and confirmed thereby. There follows from all this, with compelling logic, as its radical consequence the famous seventh and last thesis of the *Tractatus* which Wittgenstein places, un-explicated by any sub-theses, at the very end of the book:

What we cannot speak about we must pass over in silence!

This final thesis of the *Tractatus* was highly provocative in its day and indeed remains so still. Because it restricts our possible knowledge of the world strictly to that which lies within the method of the natural sciences and thereby condemns philosophy as a whole to silence:

> The correct method in philosophy would really be the following: to say nothing except what can be said, i.e. propositions of natural science – i.e. something that has nothing to do with philosophy [...] [34]

It is precisely philosophy, however, argues Wittgenstein, that has been committing, for centuries, the grave error of describing the world with many abstract words and propositions which, although they were neither tautological nor contradictory, still lacked all "meaning" in the sense of a meaning checkable against something within the real world. And as we have seen, all propositions which lack "meaning" in this specific sense of a meaning determinable within the world count, for Wittgenstein, as not just false but literally *nonsensical*:

> Most of the propositions and questions to be found in philosophical works are not false but nonsensical. [35]

"Nonsensical" as well, then, in Wittgenstein's view, are all the propositions that philosophy has produced regarding ethics and exemplary ways of acting and behaving, since these too necessarily refer to something outside the real world and are not checkable against the facts of this latter. The "Idea of the Good", for example, by which, according to Plato, we need always to orient our actions would also be, on this account, something "not just false but nonsensical", since there is no way of proving or even testing this "Idea of the Good" in terms of anything experienceable within the world we can know. Plato merely reiterates over and over the claim that "the Good" is divine and somehow related to the equally divine Ideas of "the Beautiful", "the True" and "the Just"; but he is unable to assign to this divine "Good" any concrete meaning in inner-worldly terms. But just this, as we have seen, is what all really scientific propositions need to be able to do:

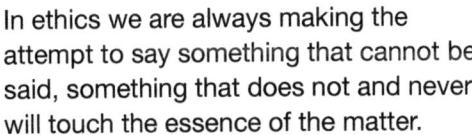

In ethics we are always making the attempt to say something that cannot be said, something that does not and never will touch the essence of the matter.

It is a priori certain that whatever definition of the good may be given, it will always be merely a misunderstanding [...] [36]

So too it is impossible for there to be propositions of ethics. Propositions can express nothing that is higher. It is clear that ethics cannot be put into words. [37]

Literally "nonsensical" for Wittgenstein too is Plato's attempt to explain the meaning of life as a testing of the soul and a drawing of it toward higher stages of development, along with the whole theory of the soul's immortality which goes along with this attempt:

[There is] no guarantee of the temporal immortality of the human soul, that is to say, of its eternal survival after death. [38]

But Wittgenstein's critique here goes still further. Because, he continues, even if the immortality of the soul were indeed a provable and proven fact, it would still not constitute an answer to the question of the meaning of life. Considered purely from a logical point of view, the particular problem of knowledge which concerns us – namely, that we do not know why we are here – would not be solved if the immortality of the soul were established but only shifted onto another level:

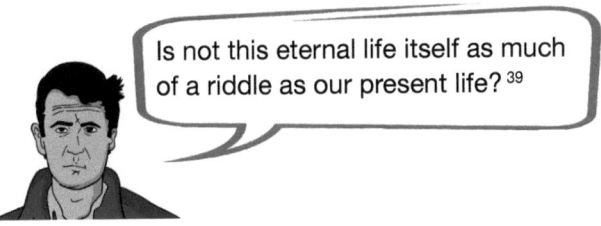

Is not this eternal life itself as much of a riddle as our present life? [39]

A logician would, for example, even as an immortal soul in Paradise still ask himself the same tormenting question as he had on earth: why is there anything at all and not rather nothing? But this question, Wittgenstein contended, can only be definitively answered from the perspective of God Himself, that is to say, from a point of view "outside the world" – which means in turn, as we have seen, that it is a *nonsensical* question, since it is not possible for anyone to ever actually adopt such a perspective. As human beings, we can only base ourselves on the facts that are accessible to us within the world. God, however, provides us with no such factual basis:

God does not reveal himself in the world. [40]

There applies here too the general principle that, regarding that which cannot be expressed in a way that makes sense and cannot be tested and confirmed by reference to the real world, one must remain silent:

Ethics, so far as it springs from the desire to say something about the ultimate meaning of life, the

absolutely good, the absolutely valuable, can be no science. What it says does not add to our knowledge in any sense. [41]

Or, stated still more clearly:

I think it is definitely important to put an end to all the claptrap about ethics: [...] whether values exist, whether the Good is definable etc. [42]

Of one thing the young Wittgenstein was absolutely certain: the various metaphysical theories produced by philosophy were, in the last analysis, no more than linguistic confusions and misunderstandings which could be avoided in future by a more logically precise use of language. And he believed that he had described and codified this more logically precise use once and for all in his *Tractatus*. Indeed, already in the preface to this key work of his youth he states with great self-confidence:

[...] The truth of the thoughts that are here communicated seems to me unassailable and definitive. [43]

Wittgenstein, Popper and the Poker

Time would show that Wittgenstein really did consider his conclusion that ethics is something one simply cannot rationally speak about to be "unassailable" – and this in the most concrete and literal sense. The intransigence with which he defended this viewpoint can be seen from a famous encounter which took place over twenty years after the publication of the *Tractatus*, in 1946, with the almost equally well-known Austrian philosopher Karl Popper. This encounter has become the stuff of legend due to the violence of the passions – so unusual among "men of science" like the two Austrian thinkers – which it is recounted, at least, to have aroused.

Popper, who had recently taken up a teaching post at the London School of Economics after spending the war years in New Zealand, had been invited up to Cambridge to give a lecture at the university's Moral Science Club on the theme of "philosophical puzzles". It was surely Wittgenstein himself who had proposed this theme, since the somewhat dismissive term "puzzle" evokes his own stance that traditional philosophical thought has consisted only in a series of confusions and contradictions arising from the misuse of language.

Popper, however – on this latter's own account of the meeting – refused to comply with this dismissive posing of the question and spoke instead on the question: "are there philosophical *problems*?", answering it in the affirmative by listing a whole series of problems which he believed fitted this description. This (according to Popper) irritated and upset Wittgenstein so much that he spent the entire lecture poking around, ever more nervously and violently, with a large metal poker in the coal-filled fireplace with which the rooms of Cambridge colleges were still, in those days, heated. Finally, he became so agitated that he cut short the invited speaker's lecture and vehemently proclaimed to the assembled students and scholars – a large number of whom were confirmed acolytes of his, since he was by now a positively legendary figure at Cambridge and in the Anglo-Saxon philosophical world in general – that all the "problems" that Popper was listing were indeed plainly cases of mistaken or nonsensical uses of language such as he had described in the *Tractatus*, emphasizing his repudiation of the speaker's views by (as Popper describes it) waving the metal fire-poker like a conductor's baton. Annoyed by the interruption, Popper replied that "if there are no such things as real philosophical problems, then (he) had no wish to be a philosopher." [44] No one, he continued, could, for example, seriously maintain that moral problems did not exist and the legitimation, or the critique of the claimed legitimacy, of moral rules was surely one of the great tasks and challenges for philosophy. For Wittgenstein this was the last straw. It was known that he considered "moral rules" to be in principle unprovable and he sprang up, pointed with the poker at Popper and demanded loudly:

Give me an example of a moral rule! [45]

Popper replied: "One shouldn't threaten an invited speaker with a poker"[46], whereupon Wittgenstein, now infuriated beyond measure, threw the poker into the corner of the room and stormed out, slamming the door.

This encounter has become the stuff of legend due to the fact that not just Wittgenstein and Popper but also several other famous philosophers of the day, such as Bertrand Russell, were present at the meeting. It has even been recounted in the form of a best-selling novel written some twenty years ago by two British journalists. Although certain details of Popper's account of the clash have been contested, the episode certainly emphasizes how passionately Wittgenstein felt about this question. His priority, right from the start, was clarity and, through clarity, a kind of redemption from the nagging questions of philosophy. Nevertheless, even the young Wittgenstein of the *Tractatus* was keenly aware that human life was impossible without an ethical or moral dimension. At bottom, the anger to which he could be provoked on this issue was an anger as much over himself as over philosophers like Popper.

This in the sense that, although Wittgenstein was indeed irritated by Popper's seeming to make the advancing of moral propositions an easy matter even though such propositions could never be grounded in any true and certain knowledge, this irritation was surely also an irritation over the fact that he had forbidden himself the very possibility of advancing any such propositions himself, since this would contravene his own injunction to "pass over in silence what we cannot speak about". Because there is no doubt but that he remained personally engaged, his whole life long, by ethical and metaphysical problems. Already in the *Tractatus* he concedes that there are problems which far exceed anything that can be formulated in scientific language:

> We feel that even when all possible scientific questions have been answered the problems of life remain completely untouched. [47]

He compares Man's desperate struggle to find answers to these most fundamental problems of life with the struggles of a fly trapped in a fly-bottle. Like this latter, Man can only flutter about tirelessly in search of some way out of his dilemmas but, just as the fly will constantly bump up against the glass of the bottle, Man will constantly find himself bumping up against the limits of language, which are the limits of what can be known:

> This running against the walls of our cage is perfectly, absolutely hopeless [...] But it is a document of a tendency in the human mind which I personally cannot help respecting deeply. [48]

In this connection Wittgenstein also points out that science, although it can explain the composition and the extension of the universe – that is to say, provide us with information about how whatever is is – cannot say anything about why there should be anything at all and not rather nothing. At the point where we are faced with this question: "why is there anything at all and not nothing?" science, says Wittgenstein, ends and "the mystical" begins:

It is not *how* things are in the world that is mystical but *that* it exists. [49]

Nor is there any logically checkable scientific answer – no "meaningful" answer in the rigorous sense of this term set by the *Tractatus* – to such questions as what makes a happy or a fulfilled life. As human beings we constantly "bump up", unfortunately, against questions that we cannot answer but that somehow impose themselves upon us just the same:

> There are, indeed, things which cannot be put into words. They *make themselves manifest*. They are what is mystical. [50]

It is possible, then, to read Wittgenstein in either of two ways. On the one hand he can be read with attention to that unsurpassable limit to all philosophizing which is set, as he insists with extreme radicality, by the logic of language itself. On the other hand he can be read with attention to all that which he did not write but which was a profound motivation prompting him to write what he did: namely, the mystical and metaphysical question regarding the meaning of life as a whole. A body of work that invites being read in both these ways may strike one almost as schizophrenic and Wittgenstein's whole life, indeed, was a torturous struggle between these two contradictory principles. In his capacity as a strict logician he burdened both himself and others with the injunction never to even try to speak about that "thing which is higher" that propositions cannot express, or about God. As a personally religious individual, however, he found himself passionately engaged by the question of the sense and meaning of our life in the world. He read Tolstoy, Pascal, Kierkegaard and many other writers who had authored writings of a mystically religious nature. When his friend and teacher, the British philosopher Russell, reminded him that he was, after all, a logician, he replied:

How can I be a logician before I'm a human being! [51]

Today's Wittgenstein scholars speak, therefore, with good reason of "the eloquent silence of Ludwig Wittgenstein" [52]. In other words: the seemingly definitive injunction directed, at the end of the *Tractatus*, to the man in search of pure, reliable knowledge that he "pass over in silence" all that concerns ethics and metaphysics is at the same time an exhortation of this same man, considered as a full human being, to go down these very roads. We may say, then, that Wittgenstein, insofar as he envisaged an ethics, envisaged an "ethics of deeds" rather than one of words: human beings, he suggested, could not, indeed, express their moral values in the form of meaningful propositions; but they could live out these moral values, bring them to realization, through what they did. Wittgenstein, however, never took up any explicit public position on ethical questions.

The *Tractatus Logico-Philosophicus* quickly rose to become a standard work of philosophical "positivism". Not only the militant "logical positivists" of the Vienna Circle but also many logicians and empiricist philosophers in the English-speaking world celebrated the little book as a monument and a manifesto against all the logical confusions besetting traditional philosophy and as the foundation stone for a new, purely positivistic approach to knowledge which would be based on "positively" demonstrable and provable facts alone and would refuse all philosophical speculation.

But if the only propositions that are to be admitted as valid are indeed propositions about facts which are both logically correctly formed and checkable against reality, then the awkward question arises of whether Wittgenstein's own discourse in the *Tractatus* is a discourse which satisfies this standard. Here, indeed, is the rub. Because what is contained in the *Tractatus* is indeed not itself a matter of "pure facts" alone. Rather it is, as its name indicates, a theoretical treatise regarding what one can and cannot know:

that is to say, an extremely abstract reflection on the theory of knowledge which could certainly never itself be (as Wittgenstein demands all true knowledge be) checked against the facts of the real world, let alone proven experimentally.

This internal contradiction of his own undertaking in the *Tractatus* could not, of course, escape so clear and strict a mind as Wittgenstein's. Consequently, we find just this problem addressed in the most disarmingly frank way in the last-but-one paragraph of the book:

My propositions serve as elucidations in the following way: anyone who understands me eventually recognizes them as nonsensical when he has used them – as steps – to climb up beyond them. [53]

The attentive reader, then – such is Wittgenstein's own intention for his book – should, once he has understood its seven theses and recognized their truth, arrive, by a final step, at the point where he applies the *Tractatus*'s demand for logical correctness and checkability against reality to the *Tractatus* itself and thus recognize that the contents of the book itself do not stand up to the test of their own logic and are, therefore, not "meaningful" in the sense which Wittgenstein himself establishes for this term.

But this is not to say (as Wittgenstein himself goes on to explain) that the book's contents are simply worthless. Once the reader has recognized that we have no legitimate reason to say anything about the world except what is based on checkable and logically coherent facts, he need pay no more attention to the particular path which led him to this recognition. The only thing that matters is that he does indeed now see the world on this new basis:

> He must, so to speak, throw away the ladder after he has climbed up it. He must transcend these propositions and then he will see the world aright. [54]

The *Tractatus* was the only philosophical work that Wittgenstein actually published during his own lifetime. Later in his life, however, he made a second philosophical discovery which was as rich in consequences as that recorded in the *Tractatus*. This was presented to the world in the posthumously published *Philosophical Investigations*. It was in this latter work that Wittgenstein discovered the true, and much more comprehensive, dimension of language and, to do justice to it, developed his theory of "language-games":

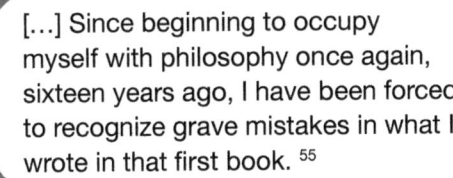

[...] Since beginning to occupy myself with philosophy once again, sixteen years ago, I have been forced to recognize grave mistakes in what I wrote in that first book. [55]

The World as Language-Game

In contrast to the "first book" referred to here, the *Tractatus*, Wittgenstein no longer defends, in the *Philosophical Investigations*, the thesis that the natural sciences alone can produce statements about the world that are concordant with the logic of language and provably true. Because language – such is the key insight of the "later Wittgenstein" who authored this second book – is far more than just the main instrument with which one can describe the world in a way that makes logical sense and is scientifically exact. Language, as it is used in everyday life, is rather a kind of "game" played between a language's speakers: a game which creates its own reality. The world, in the view of this "later Wittgenstein", consists of a great multitude of such "language-games", all of which are just as real as is that use of language which produces scientific statements:

> Review the multiplicity of language-games in the following examples, and in others: giving orders and obeying them [...] describing the appearance of an object

> [...] reporting an event [...] forming and testing an hypothesis [...] making up a story [...] play-acting [...] making a joke [...] Requesting, thanking, cursing, greeting, praying. 56

Language, that is to say, does not just describe. It can also summon to action, for example when it takes the form of orders given; or it can itself be a kind of staged action, as in play-acting.

Another demand, too, that Wittgenstein had raised in the *Tractatus* – namely, the demand that facts always be defined with words exactly appropriate to them – becomes, in the view of the older Wittgenstein, a demand impossible (at least in many cases) to fulfil, since words are often equivocal in their meanings. The proposition "this is a bank" may indeed fulfil both of the *Tractatus*'s demands in being logically well-formed and precise. It remains, however, problematical insofar as the speaker might equally well be referring to a financial institution or to a strip of land bordering a river. Words acquire their actual meaning only through the specific use that is made of them within the respective "language-games" in which they are employed.

The later Wittgenstein recognizes even a word like "five" to acquire its meaning, or meanings, only within the context of its use in one or another "language-game". When, for example, a little girl says to her mother: "I got a 'five' in arithmetic" this means she has done poorly in a test at school. But when the same girl says to her: "I'll be home at five tomorrow" she is referring rather to a time of day, and when she says "Corinna, Tina, Astrid and the Forster twins are all coming to see me on my birthday, so five altogether" it is a way of designating the entirety of the guests at a party. The same little girl might also use "five" to describe the width of her cell-phone, a seat at the cinema or the price of an ice-cream cone. It is in view of such considerations that Wittgenstein arrives at the conclusion:

The meaning of a word is its use in the language. [57]

An especially perspicuous example here is the word "game" itself. This word certainly acquires the various meanings that it bears solely and exclusively through the various contexts of its use. It would be a great mistake to suppose, warns Wittgenstein, that it is possible to define once and for all the word "game" and to assign to it just one specific correct use. Certain naïve minds, indeed, might advance the claim that "game" can be defined as, say, an amusing competition between players who, testing their skills according to certain established rules, end up as winners or losers. But if one looks a little more closely, Wittgenstein points out, this attempted definition is mere nonsense:

Consider, for example, the proceedings that we call 'games'. I mean board-games, card-games, ball-games, Olympic games and so on. What is common to them all?

[...] Are they all 'amusing'? [...] Or is there always 'winning and losing' or 'competition between players'? Think of patience. In ball-games

there is winning and losing; but when a child throws his ball at the wall and catches it again this feature has disappeared. Look at the parts played by skill and luck [...]. [58]

The essential thing in the game of chess, for example, is logical thinking; in the game of tennis it is bodily skill; and in the game of roulette pure luck alone. Solitaire is a game that one plays alone; football one that one plays in groups. The word "game", then, cannot be defined by any single overarching parameter of skill, chance or competition; rather it constantly alters the parameters of its own definition like a chameleon that changes its colour to adapt to its environment. The most that one can say is that board-games, for example, display a certain number of similarities to one another – although certain of them involve the use of dice, and thus an element of luck, while in others (such as Nine Man Morris, Chinese checkers, or chess) strategy plays a leading role. Similarly, we might note certain approximate similarities between the whole class of card-games or of ball-games. Certain approximate similarities, or overlappings, also exist between the various groups or classes of games:

We see a complicated network of similarities overlapping and criss-crossing [...] I can think of no better expression to characterize these similarities than 'family resemblances';

for the various resemblances between members of a family – build, features, colour of eyes, gait, temperament etc. – overlap and criss-cross in the same way. And I shall say 'games' form a family. [59]

There exist then in the end, for the later Wittgenstein, only certain vague "family resemblances" between the various meanings of the word "game". What is decisive, therefore, in determining this meaning in each particular case is the concrete way in which this word is used. The same, he argues, is true for almost all concepts in our various languages.

The several years that he spent as a schoolteacher allowed Wittgenstein to recognize that the demands regarding the necessity of scientific precision in all linguistic propositions that he had raised in the *Tractatus* did not, in fact, accord with the way that language is really used. Language, he discovered, proves on close analysis to be far too lively, mobile – and, consequently, imprecise – a thing for it to ever correspond precisely to the rules of logic. Instead of meditating on supposedly "ideal" linguistic formulations, Wittgenstein concluded, one must rather take ordinary, everyday language just as it is. One must observe how words are actually used. When one does this, one recognizes that the true "meanings" of words emerge always only in and through the ever shifting, ever growing and changing sets of human practices that Wittgenstein came to call "language-games".

Wittgenstein gives, at several points, clear and pre-

cise explanations of just what he means by this notion "language-game". In the first instance, he means
by it the "primitive" language-game. It is, in fact, in
our earliest childhood that we engage in our first language-games, when we learn words like "mama" and
"papa", make our first clumsy use of them, and elicit,
thereby, reactions from those who care for us:

Language-games are the forms
of language with which a child
begins to make use of words. [60]

Secondly, however, Wittgenstein also describes as
a "language-game" every other more complex type
of communication between two or more human beings, provided only that the "players" of this game
follow certain rules that have been commonly agreed
between them. These commonly-agreed rules are
necessary because without them no language-game
would be possible. Wittgenstein draws, here, a com-
parison with the game of chess. If two chess-players
fail to hold to the same set of rules and each insists
on moving his pawns, bishops, knights and castles
across the chessboard in ways that he invents or dic-

tates himself, then the game will no more work as a game than a conversation between a Spaniard and a Chinese in which both would insist on speaking only their own language would work as a conversation. But what exactly are the rules of a language-game? What presuppositions must the "players" share in order to be said to be taking part in one at all? Do these presuppositions consist only in the grammar or also in a shared knowledge of the meanings, or "family resemblances", of the words used? The first example that Wittgenstein chooses in order to explain to us the essential nature of a language-game is the especially "simple" language of people working together on constructing a building:

[The] function [of such a simple language would be] the communication between a builder A and his man B. B has to reach A building stones. There are cubes, bricks, slabs,

beams and columns. The language consists of the words 'cube', 'brick', 'slab' etc. A calls out one of these words, upon which B brings a stone of a certain shape. [61]

The language-game of these people working on constructing a building consists, then, in the first instance, in a shared knowledge of the meaning and the use of the words "cube", "brick", "slab", "beam" and "column". On looking more closely, however, one sees that it also consists in the use of certain mathematical rule-systems mastered by all the participants. This aspect proves necessary when, for example, A requires that B bring him a specific number of stones:

On being given the order 'Five slabs!' [B] goes to where the slabs are kept, says the words from one to five, takes up a slab for each word, and carries them to the builder. [62]

Furthermore, the rules and agreements constituting the language-game can be expanded and enriched during the course of the language-game itself. This happens, for example, when delivery is made to the site of the construction of a block or stone of a new shape:

B points to one of them and asks: 'what is this?' A answers: 'This is a...' Later on, A. calls out this new word, say 'arch', and B brings the stone. [63]

The language-game of the people cooperating in this job of construction, then, is characterized by a large number of shared terms peculiar to building work, such as "arch", "crossbeam", "lintel" or "telescopic support", along with a shared system of numbers and also a capacity to take up new words and concepts into the language-game where required.

Like the language of the group just described, the language-games facilitating the activities respectively of groups of atomic physicists, football-players or monks are all different and all display characteristics peculiar to themselves. Thus, the same person who develops, in the morning, together with his colleagues in an IT company, a new programming language can be found in the afternoon, as coach in a boxing club, spurring on one of his trainee boxers with words drawn from the jargon of this sport and, in the evening, amusing his infant child with imitated animal noises. That is to say, he takes part, in quick succession, in three completely different language-games. The practices that Wittgenstein calls language-games can also be characterized in terms of different milieus, different competence-levels and different ends to which action is directed. For example, the end to which the action of an IT specialist developing a new programming language is directed is clearly different from that of a trainer who is urging his trainee boxer on to victory and different also from that of the father who is trying to elicit laughter from his infant child.

Thirdly, Wittgenstein looks on a collectively spoken language as a whole – for example, the French, German or English language – as a language-game in its own right:

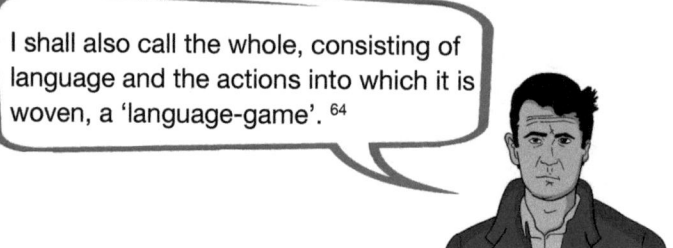

> I shall also call the whole, consisting of language and the actions into which it is woven, a 'language-game'. [64]

Wittgenstein now set about looking for the essential common characteristics that bound together and underlay all language-games. He investigated, among other aspects, grammar but had to conclude that there was no such thing as a universal basic grammar. He discovered that not only did sentence-construction – which tends in European languages to take the form "subject, predicate and object" – vary across languages but vocabulary and abstract collective terms too. There are natives of the Amazon region of Brazil, for example, whose languages contain no terms for colours nor any numbers and the sentence-construction in which allows for no sub-clauses. And even within a language-community which shares a single grammar, such as the community of French-speaking people, we see the same grammatical elements put to very different uses. The same language is used very differently, for example, in the French National Assembly in Paris than it is in the French Foreign Legion, where the French spoken surely follows a purely or primarily military logic:

It is easy to imagine a language consisting only of orders and reports in battle. [65]

Wittgenstein finally concluded, therefore, that, although the different language-games do indeed follow specific conventions and systems of rules, it is impossible to demonstrate the existence of any single essence or nature underlying and uniting all language-games:

> Here we come up against the great question that lies behind all these considerations. For someone might object against me: 'You take the easy way out! You talk about all sorts of language-games but have nowhere said what

> the essence of a language-game, and hence of language, is.' [...] And this is true. Instead of producing something common to all that we call language I am saying that these phenomena have no one thing in common [...] [66]

Instead of giving a single name to some essence common to all language-games Wittgenstein merely points, also in this case, to existing "family resemblances" and relations of "filiation". For instance, we might note a certain filiation between the military language-game, which uses such words as "officer", "order", "strategy", "campaign" and "manoeuvre", and the language-game of business and commerce, where there is often also talk of "chief executive officers", "chief financial officers", "recruiting officers", "orders", "expansion strategies" and "campaigns".

Our most important task now, then, is to discover, by the light of a large number of concrete examples, the respective meanings of words in the various different language-games. For this reason, Wittgenstein recommends that we:

Describe language-games. [67]

Wittgenstein's discovery that we live and move all our lives within different language-games may at first sound simple. We learn a language in early childhood and remain, from then on, bound into this language in terms of the meanings that we give to concepts and to the whole world around us. What makes Wittgenstein's discovery a truly explosive one, however, is his thesis that these language-games have a decisive impact on reality as we live it. We must not allow ourselves to be misled by the term "game" which

Wittgenstein uses (for reasons we have reviewed) to designate them that these language-mediated practices play only a trivial or marginal role in our existence. Rather, they are an essential part of what counts for all of us as "real".

You Are What You Speak: Words, Propositions, Forms of Life

Language-games never take place in a vacuum. Wittgenstein intensively analysed dozens, even hundreds of language-games and came to recognize that words and propositions, and the meanings that we give to these words and propositions, have a direct connection to our form of life:

The speaking of language is part of an activity, or of a life-form. [68]

This means that language-games are the reflection and the manifest expression of our familial, professional and social reality. From our earliest childhood on we become accustomed to using certain forms of expression. And these linguistic habits become firmly established, leave their mark on, and eventually entirely determine our perception of the world. One good example of this relates to the "gendering" of commonly-used nouns, a linguistic practice that never became a feature of the English language but is very common among the other languages of Europe. The German noun meaning "bridge", for instance, is a feminine noun (*die Brücke*) and, remarkably, reliable linguistic-psychological research has shown that Germans tend to attribute "feminine" characteristics (such as "slenderness" and "elegance") to bridges. Spaniards, on the other hand, in whose language the noun for "bridge" is gendered as a masculine noun, were found to spontaneously associate bridges with "masculine" attributes such as "strength" and "straightness".

The association between language and worldview becomes still more fascinating when one considers how linguistic practices affect political convictions and the sense of what is right and just. Because a language-game is not, in fact, a fixed and permanent

system but rather

> [...] Something that consists in the recurrent procedures of the game in time. [69]

Thus, language-games arise and become established in various historical eras through the repeated linguistic actions of certain "communities of action", that is to say, of specific peoples or cultures. In their function as models or patterns for social action language-games are conventions or agreements universally valid within the community in question, such as, for example, the laws and quasi-legally established customs which make up a system of law. Thus, for example, in the Middle Ages a feudal lord was able to claim, with the cry *"Jus primae noctis!"*, a right to spend the "first night" with any newly-wed bride of a serf who farmed and lived on his feudally-owned lands. Today, of course, this custom has vanished from our "language-games" and would, indeed, be thoroughly illegal. Feudal lords no longer exist and not even the bank directors and large factory-owners who have taken, in some respects, the places of these latter in our society would have the right to demand of one of their employees that he yield up to them his newly-wed wife. The concept *jus primae noctis*, then, is now forgotten. And when the use of a certain body of vocabulary, and the role played by a certain combination of words, undergoes a change, then these words also lose their power to "create a reality". Where the notion of, and word for, a certain type of law or right is forgotten:

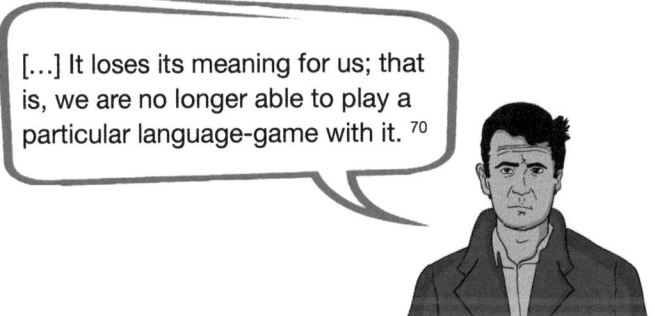

[...] It loses its meaning for us; that is, we are no longer able to play a particular language-game with it. [70]

A language-game must be constantly in use, and must be anchored by this use in society, if it is to continue to be played at all. In the histories of peoples and of cultures we see, again and again, old language-games falling into neglect and oblivion while new language-games are added. Thus, we find surviving, or half-surviving, in our language many words and phrases of very ancient date – such as "serf", "domestic slave", "lady's maid", "*lèse-majesté*", "sacrilege", or "blasphemy" – which barely play any role at all any longer in our actual speech or action. On the other hand there are also many words and phrases – such as "burn-out", "i-phone", or "digitalization" – which are widely used but have only recently been taken up into the language:

> Our language may be seen as an ancient city: a maze of little streets and squares, of old and new houses, and of houses with additions from various periods; and this surrounded by a multitude of new boroughs [...] [71]

Changes in language, then, reflect changes in our lives and in the society in which we live these lives. But Wittgenstein does not claim that each new language-game arises only out of a new, altered form of life. The contrary can also occur: a new language-game can bring about a change in our lived reality. The decisive thing as regards these changes in reality brought about by language is that all the people belonging to the respective social group or speech-community concur in their taking place. The respective language-games reflect that state of a form of social life which has already established itself as historically real. Thus, the philosopher Aristotle advocated slavery as something entirely natural, since he saw slaves as belonging to the linguistic/conceptual category of *ta onta* (mere "objects", in this case "household objects"). In terms of the language-game(s) played in most societies today it would be impossible to see things in this way. Language is, as Wittgenstein argued, a constantly developing component part of our evolution as a species:

Commanding, questioning, storytelling, chatting are as much a part of our natural history as walking, eating, drinking, playing. [72]

The significance of language-games for the personal lives of each one of us begins already with our birth. Thus, we are born into a certain family, a certain country and a certain culture:

The child learns to believe a host of things. I.e. it learns to act according to these beliefs. Bit by bit there forms a system of what is believed and

in that system some things stand unshakeably fast and some are more or less liable to shift. [73]

We are, then, existentially, from childhood on, bound into certain language-games. The first language-game is the one we play with our parents; then come language-games with siblings, other children our own age, fellow pupils, teachers, mentors, interaction with literature and media, and gradually a greater and greater participation in the language-games shared by our society as a whole. These language-games change and change us along with them:

When language-games change, then there is a change in concepts; and with the concepts the meanings of words change. [74]

Thus there grows, our whole life long, both our vocabulary and the meanings that we give to the words in it. In many cases our whole language-world is altered, and thus the whole world of our ideas and notions, and thus our basic attitude to life. Nevertheless, we remain existentially bound into the language-games of our society. We have no possibility of moving or acting outside of these. The question naturally suggests itself: 'is there really, then, not even one private and spontaneous notion that does not find itself bound into one or another social language-game and the system of following rules in which this latter consists?' But Wittgenstein's answer to this question is a clear 'no'.

Not even feelings, such as pain – which would seem, indeed, to be something that I alone am able to feel for myself – are, in Wittgenstein's view, to be considered a "private language". Because already the fact that I describe a certain feeling as "pain" presupposes that I have learnt, either in childhood or in some later language-game, to use the word "pain" with certain meanings and not with others:

What goes on within has meaning only in the stream of life. [75]

Wittgenstein considered even the free invention of completely imaginary words, or the ascription of new, private meanings to words one already knew, to be activities that were impossible, really, to carry out. If, for example, within a public language-game, I say "blood is green" the other participants can tell me that this is not the case and that, by general convention and according to generally accepted rules, the term denoting the colour of blood is "red". And if I were then to retreat to the position of trying to define blood as "green" just according to the rules of some individual private language of my own, I would then lack any point of reference or authority by which I could judge whether the rule I'd have privately established for the ascription of this term "red" was a rule which made sense or not:

Hence it is not possible to obey a rule "privately". [76]

No one can be his own sun. We remain, our whole life long, caught within the language-game of our society. If one wished to sum up Wittgenstein's central idea in a single sentence, this sentence would doubtless have to run something like this: language is far more than just a tool for making oneself understood to others because in the day-to-day language-games in which we are all involved we find condensed and concentrated all that which makes up our existence: our current form of life, our whole past life along with all past language-games practiced since our childhood, our environment, our society with its traditions, and lastly the entire historical and evolutionary development of the human species.

With his *Tractatus* Wittgenstein set about freeing the world from apparent philosophical questions which were really nonsensical, that is to say, rendering philosophy, at least in this regard, simply silent. Nonetheless, he was himself, from the very beginning, a philosopher and posed the great philosophical questions: 'what can I know?', 'what is it that determines the being of Man?', 'what is the Good and what is the Beautiful?' The answer he gives to these questions is every time the same: it is language. For it is only in the great organon of language that there are condensed together at once the gnoseological, ontological and ethical destinies of the human race. Or, expressed in less philosophically technical terms: it is only in the living medium of language that we find condensed and concentrated firstly what (limited) possibilities we have of really recognizing the facts that form the world; secondly the totality of our knowledge about what really makes up this world's essential being; and thirdly whatever we possess of ethical sense and feeling for what is good and what is just. In a word: we are language:

Look on the language-game as the *primary* thing. [77]

Of What Use Is Wittgenstein's Discovery For Us Today?

Courage to Change: Replacing One Language-Game and Form of Life With Another

But of what use to us is Wittgenstein's discovery of the profound and essential connection between language-game and "form of life"? Can we, for example, change our language-games if we find ourselves to be unhappy? Wittgenstein answers this question with a clear 'yes':

The fact that life is problematic means that your life does not fit *life's shape*. So you must change your life and, once it fits the shape, what is problematic will disappear. [78]

If our life, then, is problematic or unsatisfactory we must change the form of this life – and by "changing the form of one's life" Wittgenstein means changing our day-to-day language-games and the way(s) of living that belong to them. He did in fact do this radically and repeatedly himself, changing, not just once but several times, his profession, his nationality and the whole milieu in which he lived. As a graduate engineer he registered several patents; as an officer in the Austrian army he commanded troops in Italy; as a teacher in a small country school in Trattenbach he taught small children; as a gardener in a monastery he tended plants and then tended the wounded in a London veterans' hospital; as an architect he designed and constructed a house in Vienna; and he ended his life as a university professor in Cambridge. Moreover, these changes of place and lifestyle were not always entirely voluntary but prompted rather by the urgent need to find a new "language-game" and a new way of life corresponding to it.

He once confided to a friend, for example, that he felt that he would go mad if he spent a single day more at the university, devoting himself to philosophy. He withdrew, therefore, to Norway, where he lived alone in a wooden hut, then volunteered to fight in the First World War, and afterwards took up the post just referred to as a schoolteacher in a small village school in rural Austria. These changes of place and milieu seemed, however, to bring him peace for only short periods. His restlessness and dissatisfaction were perhaps, in part, a genetic inheritance that ran in his family. Three of his four brothers – Hans, Kurt and Rudolf – had taken their own lives and he himself suffered from recurring fits of depression in which he also contemplated suicide:

I sit astride life like a bad rider on his mount. [79]

He performed, indeed, with great personal commitment for five years his duties as a village schoolteacher; but he felt himself excluded, during this whole time, from the living "language-game" with his colleagues and with the other inhabitants of the village. Thus, he writes, in a letter dated 23rd of October 1921 to his friend Russell:

I am still at Trattenbach, surrounded, as ever, by odiousness and baseness. I know that human beings on the average are not worth much anywhere; but here

they are much more good-for-nothing and irresponsible than elsewhere. I will perhaps stay on in Trattenbach for the present year but probably not any longer because I don't get on well here even with the other teachers. [80]

Wittgenstein was, indeed, known to be strict and impatient with his pupils at the village school and, after he had given a slap to a pupil who suffered, unbeknownst to Wittgenstein, from tuberculosis and this latter lost consciousness as a result, he became the subject of a disciplinary enquiry. Although entirely exonerated, he experienced, after this incident, his teaching activity, and his isolation in the tiny rural village, as more and more of a burden and resigned shortly afterward.

He then switched residence from the tiny hamlet of only 800 souls to the great metropolis of Vienna, where he took employment in an architects studio and devoted himself, with great passion, to the design and construction of a house for his own sister. Together with his friend Engelmann he created, paying no regard to the classicizing, highly ornamental building style which at that period still dominated architecture and construction in Vienna and in Europe in general, a building of an entirely new type. Wittgenstein imposed upon the building a radically abstract and rigorously consistent architectural style which he made sure was sustained right down to the radiators and door-handles.

This prompted his sister to speak, with perhaps a note of dismay, of "logic become a house" and even Wittgenstein himself was moved to remark, in the face of the intimidatingly strict and sober impression that the finished building made:

> My house for Gretl is the product of a decidedly sensitive ear, *good* manners [...] But *primordial* life, *wild* life, striving to erupt into the open – is lacking. And so you might say: *health* is lacking. [81]

It was not just the house that lacked "wild life, striving to erupt into the open". Wittgenstein's own life was marked by the same rigour and self-control as characterized the building he created. It was only at intervals, when travelling abroad, that he was able to live out his homosexual sexual orientation. The restrictive sexual morality of the age constrained him to a life of secrecy and self-disguise. It is possible that such experiences helped to sharpen his eye for the connection between language-games and forms of life. Linguistic and social conventions, he pointed out, are of decisive importance for the flourishing, or otherwise, of a human life:

> Put a man in the wrong atmosphere and nothing will function as it should [...] Put him back into his proper element and everything will blossom and look healthy. [82]

Through his work as an architect in Vienna he made the acquaintance of the so-called "Vienna Circle", a group of Neo-Positivist philosophers who had enthusiastically celebrated his *Tractatus* and were eager to include him in their Circle's discussions. After coming, in this way, once again into contact with philosophy he decided to return to the university where he had originally studied the subject, where he became first a Fellow and then a full professor.

Wittgenstein's urging of us to "change language-games" if we are unhappy in a certain place or in the company of certain people and feel that we cannot flourish and develop under the existing circumstances is a piece of advice that remains timelessly valid and important. He concedes, nonetheless, that this is not always possible. One can be so unfortunate as to encounter, even several hundred miles away, the very same prejudices and language-games:

[...] because the clothing of our language makes everything alike. [83]

Nor can one always seek out for oneself the language-games that one prefers. Thus, for example, we are all born willy-nilly into the language-game of our parental home and live and move, during the first phase of our socialization, almost exclusively within this latter. Indeed, even once we have grown up we cannot freely choose or freely form the language-games in which we participate: in the workplace, for example, we must often just deal with the language-game going on. But, says Wittgenstein, we should, at the least, be in a position to change our environment for another if we find that we are suffering from it. And indeed, new tasks, new circles of friends, and new stimulating influences often have a liberating effect. But above and beyond this "self-help" aspect Wittgenstein's philosophical analysis of language-games also has a second, social dimension which exerts, still today, a captivating fascination.

Wittgenstein's Brilliant Linking of Language and Form of Life – Recognize the Interaction!

Each human being is the sum of all his past and present language-games. We owe our awareness of ourselves, the moral values we hold, and our entire conception of the world both to present language-games and to language-games ongoing for many centuries already. Moreover, these language-games are not simply "hanging in the air" but are inseparable from the forms of life respectively belonging to them.

Thus, the words "patrician", "plebeian" and "barbarian" belong to the language-game of the ancient Roman Empire; the words "lord" and "serf" to that of the feudal Middle Ages; and the words "negro", "redskin" and "savage" to that of the age of European colonialism (or to the "opening of the American West" insofar as this can be considered a kind of special sub-episode within this latter).

All these names and concepts correspond closely to the specific conventions and forms of life of their respective days. Within these forms of life they served, in particular, the function of justifying and legitimating the actions of those belonging to them. Thus, the obvious evil that was the subjugation and enslavement of the various peoples of Africa was linguistically minimized and rendered harmless or even benevolent by the description of its victims as "savages", "heathens" or mere "negroes" who, in their ignorant and unenlightened state, stood in urgent need of being converted and civilized:

> What people accept as a justification shows how they think and live. [84]

Today, many of these names which served to promote discrimination and subjugation have become grotesquely old-fashioned; on some there even weighs, by general consensus, a taboo so that it is hard to imagine even pronouncing them in decent, educated company. This is because, in the meantime, we have developed and adopted new language-games and new conventions:

> When language-games change, then there is a change in concepts; and with the concepts the meanings of words change. [85]

Part of the motivation, indeed, for eliminating from our current language-games, by consensual "taboos", the many racist terms which had played a role in the language-games of earlier eras, is surely to prevent a relapse into just the forms of thinking and acting that these terms had once facilitated and legitimated. The history of humanity is, in the end, nothing other than the history of the gradual transformation of language-games:

> If we imagine the facts otherwise than as they are, certain language-games lose some of their importance, while others become important. And in this way there is an alteration – a gradual one – in the use of the vocabulary of a language. [86]

The use of vocabulary, then, is in constant transformation. But the really fascinating question is: which changes first, the language-games or reality? If it is the language-games that are the first to change, this means that it is possible, by bringing about changes in the use of words, also to change reality.

We see this exemplified, in fact, in the French Revolution and the period that led up to it. Already long before the fall of the king and the other revolutionary changes that took place in the last years of the 18th century new language-games of direct relevance to these changes had begun to be played among the writers of the French Enlightenment and their public. Demands like that for "equality, freedom and brotherhood" began to be heard. Terms like "division of powers", "sovereignty of the people", "citizen" and "liberty" suddenly began to play an enormous role in social discourse. New, provocative phrases began to be taken up into the language-game, such as the question: "who should govern the people if not the people themselves?" When King Louis XVI found, in the prison where the revolutionaries imprisoned him, the works of Voltaire and Rousseau he is said to have exclaimed: "These two men have destroyed France!" Did Voltaire's and Rousseau's words really cause the old form of life to topple? Could it be the case that every such epoch-making change in real social conditions as the French Revolution is always preceded by a change in the language-game?

One thing is undeniable: as a general rule, monarchs and dictators have always attempted to spy on, control and influence the language-games of those under their sway. Censorship is as old as the written word itself. This is surely due to the fact that rulers have always known that a change in the language-game is dangerous because it can bring along with it a change in the form of life.

Wittgenstein himself never addressed at any length this fascinating question. The potentially politically explosive aspect of the phenomenon of language-games appeared to be one that did not greatly interest him. Indeed, his position was to discourage altogether all attempts to discover reasons, let alone moral or political legitimations, for one language-game's being played as opposed to another:

> Our mistake is to look for an explanation where we ought to look at what happens as a 'proto-phenomenon'. That is, where we ought to have said: this language-game is played. [87]

Wittgenstein demanded above all that words and propositions be critically analysed so that their respective meanings could be recognized with absolute clarity and all misunderstandings could be ruled out. He rejected completely the notion of making attempts to change the ongoing language-game(s) by deliberate, targeted interventions in these latter. Rather, he advanced with great emphasis the view that philosophy has, and can have, no emancipatory function, only a descriptive one:

Philosophy may in no way interfere with the actual use of language; it can, in the end, only describe it [...] It leaves everything as it is. [88]

This merely descriptive and thus completely apolitical role that Wittgenstein assigned to philosophy was especially provocative to the thinkers of the so-called "Frankfurt School", who set themselves the task of critiquing dictatorial language-games and forms of life and thus bringing about the revolutionary transformation of these latter. Herbert Marcuse, for example, the Frankfurt School writer who doubtless exercised most influence in the English-speaking intellectual world, states in his best-known work *One-Dimensional Man* that "Wittgenstein's assurance that 'philosophy leaves everything as it is' [...] exhibits, to my mind, academic sado-masochism, self-humiliation and self-denunciation".[89] It was incumbent on philosophy above all – such was Marcuse's view – to carefully observe social language-games with a view specifically to criticizing and influencing them.

Wittgenstein, however, even though he gained such insight into the potentially politically explosive connection between language-games and lived social reality, remained astonishingly apolitical. He held firmly to his position that philosophers should never try to intervene in the language-game. In his view the critical process needed to proceed in precisely the contrary direction: philosophy needed to accept the measure of its own worth to be whether or not it was using words and concepts in the same ways in which these latter were used in the language-games that make up "ordinary language". Most misunderstandings, Wittgenstein argued, arose from the fact that philosophers tended to assign to words meanings of their own choosing, high-handedly deviating further and further from the normal everyday usage of these words until, finally, total confusion reigned:

When philosophers use a word – "knowledge", "being", "object", "I", "proposition", "name" – and try to grasp the *essence* of the thing, one must always ask oneself: is the word ever actually used in this way in the language which is its original home? What *we* do is to bring words back from their metaphysical to their everyday use. [90]

One should therefore, argues Wittgenstein, give one-self the trouble to "bring back to their everyday use" all the words we find used in the work of the great philosophers and measure the philosophers' use of them against this "ordinary" use. If one did this, one would swiftly come to recognize the huge amount of nonsense that arises when philosophers reinterpret the meaning of words and concepts in the attempt to say more with these latter than one really can:

For philosophical problems arise when language *goes on holiday*. [91]

Through this high-handed redefinition of everyday words, this forcing of language to "take a holiday" from its ordinary use, philosophers hope (Wittgenstein ex-plains) to break out of the "cage of language" altogether or at least to overstep, even if it is just a little way, the limits of what language allows. But just this, Wittgen-stein says, is an illusion. Really, all that philosophers can hope to get from it is "bumps on the head":

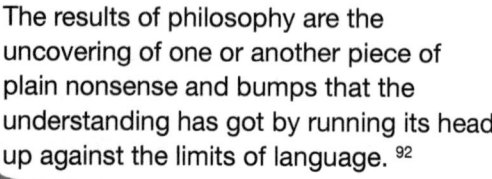

The results of philosophy are the uncovering of one or another piece of plain nonsense and bumps that the understanding has got by running its head up against the limits of language. [92]

But even if Wittgenstein, with his characteristic rigour and reserve, demanded of philosophy nothing more than that it describe the actual uses of words and propositions, he had nonetheless, with his discovery of the connection between language-game and form of life, lit the fuse of an enormous powderkeg. Because this connection was and remains highly explosive. The person who has come to recognize it will not be able to help but recognize also that language and domination are as intimately connected with one another as are language and emancipation.

Two recent philosophers as different as Derrida and Habermas, for example, have developed, each in their own way, Wittgenstein's great discovery of the link between language and form of life into philosophical discourses throwing light on the emancipatory influence of language on the way we live. Language, argues Habermas, contains, being a competence shared by the entire human species, numerous elements that link human being to human being: elements which might make possible, in the future, an entirely non-coercive discourse and thereby a non-coercive social form of life. Other recent philosophers, on the other hand, such as Marcuse, Adorno, Horkheimer and Foucault have tended to analyse rather the repressive aspects of language-use and to understand language rather as a dangerous tool for the exercise of power and domination. In both cases, however, much is owed to Wittgenstein as the thinker who first opened the door to a recognition of the enormous importance of language for our society.

"One Empire, One People, One Leader!" – Political Language-Games for the Manipulation of Forms of Life

It is one of Wittgenstein's central theses that language-games are never fixed and unchangeable; that is to say, they do not form closed systems. These games maintain their existence in a society only for so long as they are actually played. And each respective game is consolidated and solidified by its day-to-day repetition:

[...] A language-game is something that consists in the recurrent procedures of the game in time. [93]

The insight into the fact that language-games draw their force from their daily repetition is one which Wittgenstein shared with Adolf Hitler. By a strange coincidence Wittgenstein and Hitler both attended the same secondary school in the Austrian city of Linz at almost exactly the same time. Although it is unlikely that they had much personal contact with one another – Wittgenstein being one class ahead of the future dictator – it can certainly be said of both men that they paid great attention to language. But in sharp contradistinction to Wittgenstein Hitler was intent not just on analysing the connection between language and form of life but also on making use of this connection for his own purposes. Through the constant repetition of a few simple words and sentences, such as *Ein Reich! Ein Volk! Ein Fuehrer!* ("one empire, one people, one leader!") he set out to influence and transform the whole language-game of the German-speaking world. His goal was the transformation of the democratic form of life, and the canon of values which sustained it, into a form of life pervaded by the world-picture of National Socialism with its myth of a "master race in need of geographic space to fulfil its destiny". Wittgenstein himself had already recognized, with consternation, that the propositions through which a world-picture is articulated need not necessarily be true propositions, i.e. need not really correspond to the facts:

The propositions describing this world-picture might be part of a kind of mythology. [94]

Thus, by means of the massive propagandistic introduction into day-to-day German linguistic usage of words evoking "the people" (*das Volk*), the "people's health", and the "Aryan purity" and "space to expand" that were supposedly required to ensure this health – along, of course, with all the "counter-words" to these latter, evoking "enemies of the people", "parasites" and "human vermin" – Hitler was able to manipulate the German population's sense of right and wrong to such an extent that, eventually, the euthanasia of the disabled and the construction of concentration and extermination camps could be carried through without encountering any great resistance from this population.

Although it is mere speculation, then – and unlikely speculation at that – that Hitler and Wittgenstein ever had close personal contact with one another[95] the interesting fact remains that Hitler did share with Wittgenstein a keen insight into the fact that our sense of justice and injustice, our laws and everything that a particular society holds to be right or wrong, good or bad consists essentially in whatever a majority of those involved in an ongoing language-game and ongoing form of life agree on, or can be brought to agree on:

'So you are saying that human agreement decides what is true and what is false?' It is what human beings *say* that is true and

false; and they agree in the language they use. [96]

What counts as "true" or "false" is, in the end, the shared agreement of a form of life which shows itself in the language-game played by the participants in this form of life. That which human beings involved in the language-game of a certain era, or of an entire epoch, implicitly consensually agree about strikes the keynote for that which they consider to be morally right or wrong and thus provides the basic orienting principle for all their actions.

But which comes first, the implicit consensus comprised within the language-game or the explicit convergence of actions that makes up a "form of life"? That is to say: was the first thing to emerge the concrete National Socialist "form of life", in which all of Germany's real institutions were seized upon and coordinated to serve a specific political end, with the National Socialist language-game emerging only subsequently as the way of speaking and thinking that best fitted this new situation? Or did the language-game emerge first, with the form of life arising afterward to fit it? Wittgenstein describes the connection between language and concrete reality as one of reciprocal interaction and influence. He tends, however, to give priority, within this reciprocal relation, to:

> [...] Our *acting*, which lies at the bottom of the language-game. [97]

Hitler, on the other hand, assigns the initiating role to language. In his book *Mein Kampf* he deals at some length with the issue of propaganda, stating that, where propaganda is concerned: "The more modest its scientific ballast is and the more exclusively it considers the feelings of the masses the more striking will be its success [...] All effective propaganda has to limit itself to a very few points and to use them like slogans until the very last man is able to imagine what is intended by such a word. As soon as one sacrifices this basic principle and tries to become versatile, the effect will fritter away [...] All advertising, whether it lies in the field of business or of politics, will carry success by continuity and regular uniformity of application. The success of any advertising, whether in business or in politics, depends on perseverance and consistency. [98]

What gives pause for thought here is not only that Hitler did indeed achieve huge success with these methods but that strikingly similar principles and maxims – such as "memorability before variation", "keep it short", "make a promise" and "concretion before abstraction" – are to be found listed, still today, in almost all Business and Marketing Studies textbooks as the keys to effective advertising.

It has nowadays become common practice to influence and to try to change forms of life by the targeted deployment of language. Today, a whole vast army of marketing experts, campaign managers and political consultants spend their whole lives working to achieve this end. The last two victorious campaigns for the US presidency, for example – Obama's in 2008 (with re-election in 2012) and Trump's in 2016 – were both built largely upon the constant propagandistic reiteration of simple, easily memorable sentences of just three or four words conveying a highly emotionally appealing promise : Obama's "Yes, we can!" and Trump's "Make America great again!" Since both of these brief, catchy slogans were able to be so successfully implanted into the language-game of US political and social life, it must be assumed that no American election campaign will, henceforth, be able to do without some equivalent to them.

Language is important. Language is powerful. Whether it precedes reality, as a promise, or whether it gives expression to reality after the fact is a question, Wittgenstein believed, that can safely be ignored, much like the well-known question: 'which came first, the chicken or the egg?' In any case, everything that is new immediately enters into the language-game and becomes part of it:

> Something new (spontaneous, 'specific') is always a language-game. [99]

The connection recognized by Wittgenstein to exist between language and form of life has, in the end, two aspects. On the one hand, one can focus one's attention on the emancipatory character of language which is displayed, for example, where new language-games like that of the 18th-century French Enlightenment led to new and better forms of life; on the other hand, one can focus rather on the restrictive and manipulative effects exerted by language-games. Wittgenstein was, generally speaking, not a political thinker. He understood himself to be a scientist and an analyst of language alone. He would surely have rejected out of hand the question of whether specific language-games had an emancipatory or dictatorial effect upon the forms of life they were associated with as an impermissible speculative assignment of "positive" or "negative" functions to these language-games. It was fundamental to his position that language has no such single basic function:

You need to call to mind the differences between language-games. [100]

In other words, one needs always to look at the concrete, particular language-game in order to understand the meaning that it has for the particular people who play it as well as for society as a whole. Just this precise and concrete analysis of language-games, however – the using (or the omitting to use) of bold announcements, of intimidating threats, and of self-deprecating, appeasing or conciliating forms of words in one's dealings with colleagues or superiors in workplace and other contexts – has given rise to a whole new profession: the "communication coaches".

Wittgenstein's Heirs: How Communication Coaches Use Language and Grammar to Change Reality

Training in the art of speaking and arguing has been, of course, a lucrative – if not always entirely respectable – profession since ancient times. But today's "communication coaches" offer more than the teachers of rhetoric who flourished in Ancient Greece and Rome. Building on Wittgenstein's discovery that there exists a close connection between form of life and language-game, these "coaches" aim at bringing about transformations in the former by

improving the latter. Here, they are merely following out a simple insight of Wittgenstein's:

One cannot guess how a word
functions. One has to *look* at its use
and learn from that. [101]

Communication coaches do precisely this. For example, the word "perhaps" functions, in its ordinary everyday use, as a term signalling that something may
occur but also may not – or, in other words, that there
is no certainty that the event in question will come
to pass. "Perhaps", in short, stands for uncertainty,
incalculability, mere supposition. Communication
coaches, therefore, recommend that such words as
"perhaps" and "maybe" should never be used in important business meetings in association with the
speaker's own proposals or arguments, since this will
inevitably communicate a sense of great uncertainty.

For similar reasons, it is recommended that certain
grammatical forms, such as the subjunctive or the
interrogative (questioning) forms, be avoided, so
that the speaker does not appear to be assigning a

low status to him- or herself. Language-researchers have in fact discovered that women, in particular, tend to make heavy use of placative and conciliating formulations, thus running a risk of not being taken seriously. A (in the view of most communication coaches) "communicatively clumsy" phrase would be, for example: "I would add, if I may, to the discussion on this question by suggesting that we note that it will maybe do no harm here to think in a somewhat different direction. Should we not perhaps consider a new packaging for the product, or at least think about this as an option, as a way of making it more attractive to the customer?" A male speaker, socio-linguistic research suggests, would tend to present, in accordance with the rules of the "masculine language-game", the same proposal in a much more direct and even aggressive way, with some such phrase as: "Look, let me make it clear for you: if we change the packaging, we'll sell a lot more, simple as that!" The communications coach will surely urge, in such cases, female speakers to adapt themselves more to this "masculine language-game", i.e. to address the listeners directly, to use short, easily memorable phrases, and to avoid terms and grammatical forms – such as "maybe", "perhaps" and conditional and subjunctive phrase-constructions – that convey a sense of complexity and uncertainty. The woman's contribution, so goes the accepted wisdom, will then be perceived quite differently.

Adoption of the "masculine language-game" cannot, of course, be simply and unconditionally recommended to women in management and executive positions, since this language-game is also for its part characterized by many negative conventions. In the habitual language-game of men there tend also to occur certain unproductive words and grammatically useless formulations. The term "must", for example, which is especially readily and frequently used by males, tends to have the effect of restricting already beforehand all space for deviation or innovation, while at the same time creating a bad atmosphere, signalling a sense of unfreedom and subjugation which hinders the creative participation of other parties.

The ostensibly professionally expedient interventions in feminine and masculine language-games that we have briefly touched on here are just one example of how Wittgenstein's discovery of the connection between language and reality is being used, today, by a growing number of "communication" and "charisma coaches". The trend toward the growth of this new service industry is unmistakable. All leading politicians nowadays have professional aides who are able to explain to them the significance and the likely effects of various language-games and enable them to participate, with optimum success, in these latter.

Whether it be a politician attempting to win voters' support for a new system of health insurance with the slogan "Yes, we can!", a CEO pushing for the introduction of variable working-hours by claiming they will bring "more freedom for all", or a husband trying to persuade his wife to let him buy a TV with a cinema-size screen by arguing that it will not "dominate their living-room" but just make their living space "up-to-date and stylish", all will attempt, in much the manner that Wittgenstein described, to introduce the new object of their interest into the existing language-game by the argumentatively convincing choice of words and phrases, because:

Grammar tells what kind of object anything is. [102]

Recognizing the World to Be a Language-Game and Critiquing It as Such: The 'Sting in the Tail' of Wittgenstein's Descriptive Analysis of Language

All philosophy is a critique of language [...] [103]

Wittgenstein urges us to practice the critique of language. By this he means the critical analysis of words and propositions as they are used against the background of their respective forms of life. The postmodern French philosopher Derrida took up and further developed this language-critical approach of Wittgenstein's. Derrida concurred entirely with Wittgenstein's conclusion that words and propositions acquire their meanings only from the language-games in which they are used and that these meanings, therefore, are inseparably linked with specific forms of life. Thus, specific languages, such as French, Chinese or Arabic, exist in close relation with certain cultures, religions and traditions. As we have seen, Wittgenstein came to see each language as a living whole: a language-game which maintained and preserved many names and concepts which had existed in it since earliest times while also drawing in new names and concepts, much in the way in which an ancient city continues to grow:

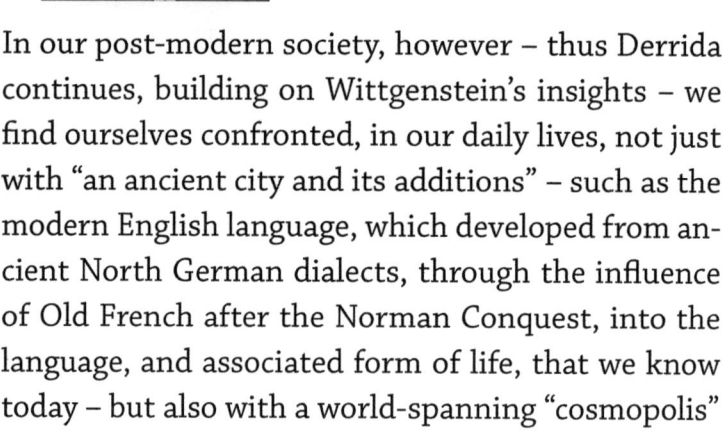

Our language may be seen as an ancient city: a maze of little streets and squares, of old and new houses, and of houses with additions from various periods; and this surrounded by a multitude of new boroughs [...] [104]

In our post-modern society, however – thus Derrida continues, building on Wittgenstein's insights – we find ourselves confronted, in our daily lives, not just with "an ancient city and its additions" – such as the modern English language, which developed from ancient North German dialects, through the influence of Old French after the Norman Conquest, into the language, and associated form of life, that we know today – but also with a world-spanning "cosmopolis" consisting in a confusing juxtaposition of the most various language-games and cultures.

Whereas in past centuries the only news we got of distant, foreign cultures and of the language-games that constituted them came to us through adventurous and highly exceptional world-travellers like Marco Polo, in this last half-century these language-games have begun to come directly and massively into contact with one another. This "globalization" of our experience has often provoked fear and mistrust. Derrida compares this fear engendered by the encounter with alien language-games with the Biblical story of "the Tower of Babel" and the "confusion of tongues" that followed from it. The Old Testament tells of how men of ancient times attempted to build "a tower that would reach to Heaven" and how this project foundered on the confusion caused by the many different languages spoken by the various groups participating in it. But it is time, so argues Derrida, for the human race to finally overcome and abandon this archetypal image of threat and destruction.

The encounter of different language-games in our present post-modernity then, however strange and disorienting an impression these different language-games might make on one another, should no longer be experienced as a source of anxiety, and certainly not as a "clash of civilizations", but rather as a great opportunity. Derrida urges us, instead of yielding to mistrust, to embrace the opening of our own language-games to others and to attempt to establish an intercultural language-game comprising all the globe's different forms of life. What is meant by this is not that the whole world should learn English and use this ostensibly "world language" to override, in their communications and interactions, the traditional languages and religions that make up their own cultures but rather that new words, propositions and meanings should arise which do justice to players of all language-games and to practitioners of all forms of life. There must, essentially, come into existence a new, expanded language-game for our present expanded age – something that, in terms of Wittgenstein's vision, is entirely possible:

[...] New types of language – new language-games, as we may say – come into existence and others become obsolete and get forgotten.[105]

In order to overcome and forget one's own locally restricted language-game, argues Derrida, one must take steps to dissolve, or at least render fluid and flexible, those names and concepts which stand in the way of an opening to the "outside". He suggests, for example, with reference to the case of Israel, that the phrase "chosen people" should now – despite the fact that it has been anchored in the language-game of the Hebrew language and in the form of life of the Jewish people for over 2000 years – be re-interpreted in such a way as to extend its meaning to all the peoples of the earth. Because otherwise, Derrida warns, in that expanded global language-game which characterizes our present era, participants in this game belonging to other cultural milieus could feel themselves to be looked on as "not chosen" and thus as not accepted as an equal partner in dialogue.

Many old concepts made, at certain points in ancient history, historical and mythological sense but represent, today, unnecessary obstacles to progress. Derrida, as a Frenchman of Jewish background – i.e. someone who was raised in two cultures and two language-games – had an especially acute perception for the ways in which grammar can both exclude and draw together. It was his view that all names and concepts likely to establish or reinforce hierarchical structures need, at our present point in history, to be abandoned.

Derrida's vision of the freeing of post-modern language-games from old dogmas and of their opening-up for a truly global discourse is, in essence, just a further development of Wittgenstein's central idea. Wittgenstein, indeed, had rejected the idea of a targeted intervention in existing language-games but had recognized, nonetheless, the possibility in principle of such an intervention insofar as he recognized the reciprocal dependence and influence of language-game and form of life:

[...] Certain language-games lose some of their importance, while others become important. And in this way there is an alteration – a gradual one – in the use of the vocabulary of a language. [106]

Is Derrida's vision of a "global language game" in which all cultures, religions and forms of life might play an equal part really a vision that might one day become reality? Are we already on our way to its doing so? Wittgenstein would certainly not have gone so far as to say so. He would most likely, with his characteristic rigor, have rejected even the question as to a possible "single global language-game" as impermissible speculation. His primary aim in all his analyses was simply to better understand the use of words, their meanings, and thus the ways in which we perceive the world. But precisely his desperate struggle with these problems, his own "running up against the limits of language", made him a pioneer anticipating and preparing our own "post-modern" human predicament. Whether he intended to do so or not, he undoubtedly altered, with his critique of language, the way in which we, contemporary humankind, perceive ourselves and our situation.

Since Wittgenstein no one, anywhere in the world, is any longer able to advance a verbal proposition "innocently", that is, with a sense of doing something self-evident, natural and entirely unproblematic. "Purely propositional" speech is something we can now no longer believe in. Wittgenstein has put, as it were, a "sting in the tail" of even the most simple and naïve act of language. Since his *Philosophical Investigations* we are all aware that the meaning of every phrase, be it true or false, is inseparably linked to an extensive sub- and superstructure of religious, ideological and material traits and characteristics making up the specific form, or forms, of life to which the person speaking it belongs. Since Wittgenstein, no word is ever any longer just a word nor any sentence just a sentence.

Whoever really absorbs and internalizes this truth necessarily becomes permanently keenly attentive to all the language-games going on around him, be it in his family, in his circle of friends or in the wider society. He listens with a more critical ear than he might otherwise have done to the formulations he hears in daily news broadcasts and may even have more difficulty than he once did in believing blindly in his own statements and in demanding that others accept unconditionally the validity and the rightness of these statements. Because he is aware now that the fact that these statements have meaning at all is due only to the spatially and temporally limited language-game of the specific form of life to which he belongs.

He is aware also that the broadening of this language-game, and the making of it a language-game open to other interpretations, is always a possibility. Even where language-games between human beings, peoples and civilizations follow long-established grammatical rules, conventions and incrusted shared understandings, something new can occur at any time:

When language-games change, then there is a change in concepts; and with the concepts the meanings of words change. [107]

Concepts (words, meanings) such as "redskin", "serf", "sub-human", "the white man's burden", "heretic", "witch", "heathen" or "infidel" will increasingly lose their meaning and, at some point, vanish from the language-game entirely. Their place will perhaps be taken by concepts such as "human dignity", "blue planet", or others as yet unknown to us. Larger-scale language-games and forms of life are growing and gaining ground. Wittgenstein has shown us, in the most impressive possible way, that a "language-game", despite all the old rules and handed-down conventions which necessarily make up part of what it is, amounts in the end to much more than simply a repetitive exchange of existing information:

You must bear in mind that the language-game is, so to say, something unpredictable [...] It is there – like our life. [108]

Bibliographical References

1   Ludwig Wittgenstein, *Tractatus Logico-Philosophicus*, translated by
    D.F. Pears and B.F. McGuinness, Routledge and Kegan Paul, Oxford
    and New York, 1974, p. 3
2   Ibid. p. 68
3   Ludwig Wittgenstein, A Lecture on Ethics in J.C. Klagge,
    A. Nordmann (eds) Philosophical Occasions 1912-1951,
    Hackett Publishing Company, Indianapolis, Indiana, p. 44.
4   Ludwig Wittgenstein, *Philosophical Investigations* (The German
    Text with a Revised English Translation) translated by
    G.E.M Anscombe, Blackwell Publishers, Oxford, 2001, p. 90 (English).
5   Ludwig Wittgenstein, *Tractatus Logico-Philosophicus*, translated by
    D.F. Pears and B.F. McGuinness, Routledge and Kegan Paul, Oxford
    and New York, 1974, p. 23
6   Ibid.
7   Ludwig Wittgenstein, *Philosophical Investigations* (The German Text
    with a Revised English Translation) translated by G.E.M Anscombe,
    Blackwell Publishers, Oxford, 2001, p. 189 (English).
8   Ibid. p. 10 (English)
9   Hermine Wittgenstein, Family Memories, quoted in
    Nicole L. Immler, Das Familiengedaechtnis der Wittgensteins,
    Transcript Verlag, Bielefeld, 2011, p. 32.
10 Ludwig Wittgenstein, *Tractatus Logico-Philosophicus*, translated by
    D.F. Pears and B.F. McGuinness, Routledge and Kegan Paul, Oxford
    and New York, 1974, p. 89
11 Ibid.
12 Ibid. p. 86.
13 Ibid. p. 4
14 Ludwig Wittgenstein, *Philosophical Investigations* (The German Text
    with a Revised English Translation) translated by G.E.M Anscombe,
    Blackwell Publishers, Oxford, 2001, p. 141 (English).

15   Ludwig Wittgenstein, Culture and Value, (Vermischte Bemerkungen) Bilingual Edition, ed. by G. H. von Wright, Blackwell, Oxford, 1998, p. 48 (English).

16   Ludwig Wittgenstein, *Tractatus Logico-Philosophicus*, translated by D.F. Pears and B.F. McGuinness, Routledge and Kegan Paul, Oxford and New York, 1974, p. 5.

17   Ibid.

18   Ibid. p. 9

19   Ibid.

20   Ludwig Wittgenstein, Notebooks 1914-16, edited by G.H. von Wright and G.E.M Anscombe, Basil Blackwell, Oxford, 1961 p. 7 (English).

21   Ludwig Wittgenstein, *Tractatus Logico-Philosophicus*, translated by D.F. Pears and B.F. McGuinness, Routledge and Kegan Paul, Oxford and New York, 1974, p. 12

22   Ibid.

23   Ludwig von Wittgenstein, Notebooks 1914-1916, edited by G.H von Wright and G. E. M. Anscombe, (German Text with Facing English Translation) Basil Blackwell, Oxford, 1961, p. 7 (English)

24   Ludwig Wittgenstein, *Tractatus Logico-Philosophicus*, translated by D.F. Pears and B.F. McGuinness, Routledge and Kegan Paul, Oxford and New York, 1974, p. 24.

25   Ibid. p. 23.

26   Ibid. p. 43

27   Ibid. p. 26

28   Ibid.

29   Ibid. p. 86

30   Ibid. p. 42

31   Ibid. p. 57

32   Ibid. p. 30

33   Ibid. p. 89

34   Ibid.

35   Ibid. p. 22

36   Wittgenstein and the Vienna Circle, edited by F. Waismann and B. McGuinness, Basil Blackwell, Oxford, 1979, p. 69.

37   Ludwig Wittgenstein, *Tractatus Logico-Philosophicus*, translated by D.F. Pears and B.F. McGuinness, Routledge and Kegan Paul, Oxford and New York, 1974, p. 86.

38   Ibid. p. 87

39   Ibid.

40   Ibid. p. 88

41   Ludwig Wittgenstein, A Lecture on Ethics in J.C. Klagge,
     A. Nordmann (eds) Philosophical Occasions 1912-1951,
     Hackett Publishing Company, Indianapolis, Indiana, p. 44.

42   Wittgenstein and the Vienna Circle, edited by F. Waismann and
     B. McGuinness, Basil Blackwell, Oxford, 1979, pp. 68-69

43   Ludwig Wittgenstein, *Tractatus Logico-Philosophicus*, translated by
     D.F. Pears and B.F. McGuinness, Routledge and Kegan Paul, Oxford
     and New York, 1974, p. 4.

44   Karl Popper, Unended Quest : An Intellectual Autobiography,
     Routledge, London, 1992, pp. 122-123.

45   Ibid.

46   Ibid.

47   Ludwig Wittgenstein, *Tractatus Logico-Philosophicus*, translated by
     D.F. Pears and B.F. McGuinness, Routledge and Kegan Paul, Oxford
     and New York, 1974, p. 88.

48   Ludwig Wittgenstein, A Lecture on Ethics in J.C. Klagge,
     A. Nordmann (eds), Philosophical Occasions 1912-1951,
     Hackett Publishing Company, Indianapolis, Indiana, p. 44.

49   Ludwig Wittgenstein, *Tractatus Logico-Philosophicus*, translated by
     D.F. Pears and B.F. McGuinness, Routledge and Kegan Paul, Oxford
     and New York, 1974, p. 88.

50   Ibid. p. 89.

51   Ludwig Wittgenstein, Letters to Russell, Keynes and Moore, edited by
     G. H. von Wright, Basil Blackwell, Oxford, 1974, p. 58.

52   See, for example, Axel Hutter Die Verwandtschaft von Philosophie
     und Religion in Philosophie und Religion edited by Jens Halfwassen
     et al, Heidelberg 2011 (untranslated) : "The silence that Wittgenstein
     demands at the end (of the 'Tractatus') allows itself to be recognized
     as a form of 'eloquent silence'" (p. 16)

53   Ludwig Wittgenstein, *Tractatus Logico-Philosophicus*, translated by
     D.F. Pears and B.F. McGuinness, Routledge and Kegan Paul, Oxford
     and New York, 1974, p. 89.

54   Ibid.

55   Ludwig Wittgenstein, *Philosophical Investigations* (The German Text
     with a Revised English Translation) translated by G.E.M Anscombe,
     Blackwell Publishers, Oxford, 2001, p. x (Preface) (English).

56 Ibid. p. 10 (English)

57 Ibid. p. 18 (English)

58 Ibid. p. 27 (English)

59 Ibid. pp. 27-28 (English)

60 Ludwig Wittgenstein, The Blue and Brown Books : Preliminary Studies for the *Philosophical Investigations*, Basil Blackwell, Oxford, 1969, p. 17.

61 Ibid. p. 77

62 Ibid. p. 79

63 Ibid. pp. 81-82

64 Ludwig Wittgenstein, *Philosophical Investigations* (The German Text with a Revised English Translation) translated by G.E.M Anscombe, Blackwell Publishers, Oxford, 2001, p. 4 (English).

65 Ibid. p. 7 (English)

66 Ibid. p. 27 (English)

67 Ibid. p. 116 (English)

68 Ibid. p. 10 (English)

69 Ludwig Wittgenstein, On Certainty (The German Text with English Translation) edited by G.E. Anscombe and G.H. von Wright, Basil Blackwell, Oxford, 1969, p. 68 (English).

70 Ludwig Wittgenstein, *Philosophical Investigations* (The German Text with a Revised English Translation) translated by G.E.M Anscombe, Blackwell Publishers, Oxford, 2001, p. 24 (English).

71 Ibid. p. 7 (English).

72 Ibid. p. 11 (English)

73 Ludwig Wittgenstein, On Certainty (The German Text with English Translation) edited by G.E. Anscombe and G.H. von Wright, Basil Blackwell, Oxford, 1969, p. 21 (English).

74 Ibid. p. 66 (English).

75 Wittgenstein, Last Writings on the Philosophy of Psychology, Volume Two, (ed. by G.H. von Wright and Heikki Nyman), Basil Blackwell Oxford, 1982, p. 30.

76 Ludwig Wittgenstein, *Philosophical Investigations* (The German Text with a Revised English Translation) translated by G.E.M Anscombe, Blackwell Publishers, Oxford, 2001, p. 69 (English).

77 Ludwig Wittgenstein, *Philosophical Investigations* (The German Text with a Revised English Translation) translated by G.E.M Anscombe, Blackwell Publishers, Oxford, 2001, p. 141 (English).

78 Ludwig Wittgenstein, Wittgenstein's Nachlass : Text and Facsimile Version. The Bergen Electronic Edition, Oxford University Press, 2000 ; MS 118, 17r – 17v.

79 Ludwig Wittgenstein, Culture and Value (Vermischte Bemerkungen) Bilingual Edition, ed. by G. H. von Wright, Blackwell, Oxford, 1998, p. 42 (English).

80 Ludwig Wittgenstein, Letters to Russell, Keynes and Moore, edited by G. H. von Wright, Basil Blackwell, Oxford, 1974, pp. 94-95.

81 Ludwig Wittgenstein, Culture and Value (Vermischte Bemerkungen) Bilingual Edition, ed. by G. H. von Wright, Blackwell, Oxford, 1998, p.

43 (English).

82 Ibid. p. 48 (English).

83 Ludwig Wittgenstein, *Philosophical Investigations* (The German Text with a Revised English Translation) translated by G.E.M Anscombe, Blackwell Publishers, Oxford, 2001, p. 191 (English).

84 Ibid. p. 90 (English).

85 Ludwig Wittgenstein, On Certainty (The German Text with English Translation) edited by G.E. Anscombe and G.H. von Wright, Basil Blackwell, Oxford, 1969, p. 10 (English).

86 Ibid.

87 Ludwig Wittgenstein, *Philosophical Investigations* (The German Text with a Revised English Translation) translated by G.E.M Anscombe, Blackwell Publishers, Oxford, 2001, p. 141 (English).

88 Ibid. p. 42.

89 Herbert Marcuse, One-Dimensional Man : Studies in the Ideology of Advanced Industrial Society (Boston, Beacon Press, 1966) p. 173

90 Ludwig Wittgenstein, *Philosophical Investigations* (The German Text with a Revised English Translation) translated by G.E.M Anscombe, Blackwell Publishers, Oxford, 2001, p. 41 (English).

91 Ibid. p. 16 (English)

92 Ibid. p. 41 (English)

93 Ludwig Wittgenstein, On Certainty (The German Text with English Translation) edited by G.E. Anscombe and G.H. von Wright, Basil Blackwell, Oxford, 1969, p. 68 (English).

94 Ibid.p. 15 (English)

95 One particularly adventurously speculative account of such "close personal contact" between the two later-famous men as schoolboys is Kimberley Cornish's 1998 book The Jew of Linz (Century Books, 1998).

The consensus in scholarly responses to Cornish's book, however, has been that Cornish offers absolutely no real evidence for his claim that an encounter with a teenage Wittgenstein at this time was a – and even the – decisive event in the formation of Hitler's antisemitic obsession.

96 Ludwig Wittgenstein, *Philosophical Investigations* (The German Text with a Revised English Translation) translated by G.E.M Anscombe, Blackwell Publishers, Oxford, 2001, p. 75 (English).

97 Ludwig Wittgenstein, On Certainty (The German Text with English Translation) edited by G.E. Anscombe and G.H. von Wright, Basil Blackwell, Oxford, 1969, p. 28 (English).

98 Adolf Hitler, Mein Kampf, Reynal and Hitchcock, New York, 1941, pp. 233-240

99 Ludwig Wittgenstein, *Philosophical Investigations* (The German Text with a Revised English Translation) translated by G.E.M Anscombe, Blackwell Publishers, Oxford, 2001, p. 191 (English).

100 Ibid. p. 84 (English)

101 Ibid. p. 93 (English)

102 Ibid. p. 99 (English)

103 Ludwig Wittgenstein, *Tractatus Logico-Philosophicus*, translated by D.F. Pears and B.F. McGuinness, Routledge and Kegan Paul, Oxford and New York, 1974, p. 23

104 Ludwig Wittgenstein, *Philosophical Investigations* (The German Text with a Revised English Translation) translated by G.E.M Anscombe, Blackwell Publishers, Oxford, 2001, p. 7 (English).

105 Ibid. p. 10 (English).

106 Ludwig Wittgenstein, On Certainty (The German Text with English Translation) edited by G.E. Anscombe and G.H. von Wright, Basil Blackwell, Oxford, 1969, p. 66 (English).

107 Ibid. p. 10 (English).

108 Ibid. p. 73 (English).

Already published in the same series:

Walther Ziegler
Camus in 60 Minutes
ISBN 9783741227738

Walther Ziegler
Freud in 60 Minutes
ISBN 9783741227707

Walther Ziegler
Hegel in 60 Minutes
ISBN 9783741227677

Walther Ziegler
Heidegger in 60 Minutes
ISBN 9783741227752

Walther Ziegler
Kant in 60 Minutes
ISBN 9783741226373

Walther Ziegler
Marx in 60 Minutes
ISBN 9783741227691

Walther Ziegler
Nietzsche in 60 Minutes
ISBN 9783752803822

Walther Ziegler
Platon in 60 Minutes
ISBN 9783741227615

Walther Ziegler
Sartre in 60 Minutes
ISBN 9783741227653

Walther Ziegler
Rousseau in 60 Minutes
ISBN 9783741227622

Walther Ziegler
Smith in 60 Minutes
ISBN 9783741227721

Walther Ziegler
Rawls in 60 Minutes
ISBN 9783750424050

Coming soon in the same series:

Walther Ziegler
Adorno in 60 Minutes

Walther Ziegler
Arendt in 60 Minutes

Walther Ziegler
Bacon in 60 Minutes

Walther Ziegler
Foucault in 60 Minutes

Walther Ziegler
Habermas in 60 Minutes

Walther Ziegler
Hobbes in 60 Minutes

Walther Ziegler
Popper in 60 Minutes

Walther Ziegler
Schopenhauer in 60 Minutes

The author:

Dr Walther Ziegler is academically trained in the fields of philosophy, history and political science. As a foreign correspondent, reporter and newsroom coordinator for the German TV station ProSieben he has produced films on every continent. His news reports have won several prizes and awards.He has also authored numerous books in the field of philosophy. His many years of experience as a journalist mean that he is able to present the complex ideas of the great philosophers in a way that is both engaging and very clear. Since 2007 he has also been active as a teacher and trainer of young TV journalists in Munich, holding the post of Academic Director at the Media Academy, an institute of higher education that offers film and TV courses at its base directly on the site of the major European film production company Bavaria Film.